SHEILA ROWBOTHAM

Woman's Consciousness, Man's World

PENGUIN BOOKS

Penguin Books Ltd, Harmondsworth, Middlesex, England
Viking Penguin Inc., 40 West 23rd Street, New York, New York 10010, U.S.A.
Penguin Books Australia Ltd, Ringwood, Victoria, Australia
Penguin Books Canada Limited, 2801 John Street, Markham, Ontario, Canada L3R 1B4
Penguin Books (N.Z.) Ltd, 182–190 Wairau Road, Auckland 10, New Zealand

First published in Pelican Books 1973
Reprinted 1974, 1975, 1976, 1977, 1979, 1981, 1983, 1986

Made and printed in Great Britain by
Hazell Watson & Viney Limited,
Member of the BPCC Group,
Aylesbury, Bucks
Set in Linotype Plantin

Contents

Acknowledgements

I would like to thank the following for reading and criticizing this book while it was being written:

Sally Alexander, Val Charlton, Val Clarke, Sharon Collins, Anna Davin, Suzie Fleming, Hermione Harris, Juliet Mitchell, Laura Mulvi, Jean McCrindle, Ursula Owen, Amanda Sebestyen, Sue Sharpe, Sue Vickery, Michelene Wandor, Liz and Lucy Waugh; also, Ann Scott who typed it as well, and David Widgery whose love of words and their weaving persuaded me to write as I fancied, and take my own assertions about the redefinitions of personal and political seriously enough to include myself in Part 1.

For help with Part 2 thanks to Stephen Bodington who set off the train of thought, to Roberta Hunter-Henderson whose paper at the Sheffield Women's Liberation Conference in summer 1970 also contributed, to Françoise Ducroq whose notes I read on the family.

For criticism of the original draft of Part 2, which was written as a paper for a seminar held by members of the Institute of Race Relations in spring 1971, I would like to thank some of the people who attended the seminar, particularly Bill Tabb; also members of Sheffield and Leeds Women's Liberation Groups, a meeting of London Women's Liberation Groups, and Arsenal Workshop Group, who helped me to sort my ideas out and make my writing clearer. For suggestions and additions to the original paper I am also indebted to Bob Rowthorn and Jean Gardiner who gave me the confidence to make economic pronouncements. For help with Chapter 6, thanks to May Hobbs, Jean Wright and other members of the Night Cleaners Campaign, also to Gertie Roche for information about the Leeds clothing strike, and Audrey Wise for the letter I have quoted and advice and ideas about women and trade unions.

The bulk of this book was written in the summer of 1971 as part of *Women, Resistance and Revolution*. It grew too big and had to be cut apart and lead its own life. I finished revising it in the spring of 1972. In the process I was assimilating the ideas of women in women's liberation not only in Britain but in France, Germany, Holland,

Australia, Japan, Italy, Sweden and of course the USA, often without realizing where exactly thoughts came from. So although I am responsible for what I have made, the making of it has been the ideas and actions of the women's movement. This does not mean of course that everyone in women's liberation will agree with this book or even with sections of it. In order to show there are several approaches to the problems I have discussed and to enable anyone who is interested to pursue them further I have included a list of pamphlets and articles published after this was written.

Introduction

Bewilderment and mystery surrounded the birth of women's liberation. It seemed to come out of an ideological lacuna belonging neither to previous feminism nor to Marxism. Orphan-like it had apparently sprung up from nowhere in particular, unashamed by its lack of origins or kin. Feminists and Marxists alike were convinced that when it grew up, and became sensible like them, it would shed its ill-defined 'absurdities'. Both claimed that whatever it was the women in the new movement were trying to say, the essential points had been fully covered by their respective traditions in a much more political and worked-out fashion long before. Older women who could remember feminism were irritated by the claims that women's liberation was something new. Marxists were impatient of the claim that middle-class women were oppressed and confident that feminism was a deviation from class politics. The distortion both of the feminist past and of the part women have played in revolutions confused the whole discussion. In the process the specific crannies and fissures of social experience which had given rise to women's liberation were neglected.

In fact women's liberation does have strands of the older equal-rights feminism, and it also has a persistent revolutionary socialist connection, but it is something more than either of these.[1] It has given expression to a new consciousness among women and it came out of a social reality which is peculiar to the kind of life possible in advanced capitalism. Its immediate political context was the inchoate radicalism of the student left in the late sixties, and the specifically female contradictions confronted by women who entered higher education.[2] However, the new feminist consciousness has deeper and less obvious origins.

1. See Juliet Mitchell, *Woman's Estate*, Penguin, 1971.
2. See ibid. Apart from Juliet Mitchell's book discussion about the con-

This book is an attempt to describe the form which this consciousness has taken, and some of the social changes which forced its growth. In trying to describe what is specific to the female consciousness which has appeared in women's liberation, I am not suggesting that biology is destiny. I do not believe that women or men are determined either by anatomy or economics, though I think both contribute to a definition of what we can be and what we have to struggle to go beyond. An emergent female consciousness is part of the specific sexual and social conjuncture, which it seeks to control and transform. But its very formation serves to change its own material situation.

In the first two chapters I touch on some of the ways of thinking which acted as a block upon the emergence of a revolutionary feminism: the failure of both the rational equal-rights feminism of the suffragette era, and the Marxist orthodoxy of Stalin's rule, to come to terms with the insights of Freudianism and cultural studies of non-capitalist societies. More personally I have tried to describe the caricature of feminism transmitted into my own post-war adolescence, and the awkwardness in the desiccated revolutionary tradition of the mid sixties in Britain which made it particularly difficult to use Marxism as a creative and living force. My generation, who came to left politics immediately before the eruption of the student revolt, inherited a Marxism which had only continued in the western capitalist countries as a defensive body of orthodoxy surrounded by protective walls, encrusted with fear, stiff with terror, brittle with bitterness, aching with disillusionment. There are many ways of trying to understand sectarianism. I have simply brought into relief my own bemused encounter, like a child who finds a penny and covering it with paper brings the imprint into view by scratching it with a lead pencil. Less

---

nection between women's liberation and the student left has been mainly in the American context. See for example articles in *Radical America*, Vol. 4, February 1970, the section on 'Up from Sexism' in *Sisterhood is Powerful*, ed. Robin Morgan. On France see 'Libération des femmes, année zéro', *Partisans*, July–October 1970. For Italy see 'An Open Letter to our Sisters Abroad' in *Women Now*, Vol. 1 no. 2. See also, on Britain, Ellen Malos' 'Notes on the History of the Women's Liberation Movement' in *Enough*, Bristol Women's Liberation Group.

tangibly there were too the popular permutations of anti-rationalism, and the images of masculinity and femininity, picked up, turned round, rolled out, packaged, flickering, throbbing through rock music, films and TV. But the things which were called political were apparently irreconcilably dissociated from personal life.

In 'Through the Looking-Glass' I am trying to examine the way society communicates to the individual. It is not that the perception of women is unique. On the contrary, oppression has many common features – and thus rebellion can locate and connect itself. For example, the demands of both the working class and of black liberation to control and define their existence now and in the past, their resistance to the appropriation of their labour, their language, their gestures, their dreams, have helped many women to wonder where they are in '*man*kind' and 'hu*man*ity'. Women are still divorced from these words. We are not included in the notion now of what is human. Nor are we part of the alternatives made by men. The idea of militant dignity exists in the word 'manhood' or in the idea of 'virility' or the solidarity of 'brotherhood'. Women have only the neutered dignity men have allowed the women they have called 'good'. The indignity of femininity has been internalized for millennia. Sisterhood demands a new woman, a new culture, and a new way of living. The intimate oppression of women forces a redefinition of what is personal and what is political.

The immediate response when you grasp this is to deny all culture, because everything that has been created, all universal values, all notions of what we are, have been made in a society in which men have been dominant. But the problem created by simply rejecting everything that is, and inverting existing male values to make a female culture out of everything not male, is that the distortions of oppression are perpetuated.

The elevation of the family and domestic values in opposition to 'materialism' or 'competition' nearly always takes a politically reactionary form. Just as the elevation of 'motherhood' or of a feminine culture which is merely the reverse of existing male-dominated culture is also reactionary in effect. By making the family, motherhood or feminine culture into an abstracted ideal, the real connections between the distortion of human relations in the family and in capitalist commodity production are obscured. By isolating and freezing one aspect of human relations a utopianism of the right or of the left is produced. The utopianism of the right dreams of a world of comfort and security, with women in the home, and every man in his proper station. Sexual roles are distinct and clear cut, as are class and racial roles. The development of capitalism itself makes such a phoney harmony unreal. In a different way there is a tendency in the women's movement to elevate the existing consciousness of women, to demand change in the social relationship of the sexes by an act of will, and to isolate women as a group from men. The dream of harmony can be acted out between women because it is assumed women have been mysteriously uncorrupted by living in the real world. However, women have not been unaffected by capitalism and oppression. The idealization of women is incongruous in a revolutionary feminist movement. It belongs rather to the sentimentalism which elevates powerless people into innocents. Innocence is impossible when people have never had the choice of becoming corrupt by dominating others. Not only is 'woman' abstracted from society in the here-and-now, but the different possibilities for men and women are held to be biological and psychological in origin, and thus the need to transform the social relations between all human beings is ignored.

The act of oppression not only disfigures the oppressor, it also maims the oppressed. A new culture cannot be made *only* out of the heads of those who rebel. Exhortation to liberation merely as an act of will can harden into a stereotype which itself becomes a block on the self-activity of the oppressed.

> 'she did suffer, the witch;
> trying to peer round the looking
> glass, she forgot
> someone was in the way.'[3]

We have to make ourselves not as a projected abstract ideal, but out of the shapes of here and now. The barriers which confront us are real, not merely the conjurings of our imagination. We

3. Michelene, 'Reflexion', *Shrew*, May 1971, p. 4.

cannot bypass the long making of a new society simply by inventing a liberated female culture, intact out of time and space, unaffected by the social relations which exist around us. The movement between conception and action, culture and social revolution, is partial, laboured, and painfully slow. But it is the only way we can heave ourselves into the future.

Oppression is not an abstract moral condition but a social and historical experience. Its forms and expression change as the mode of production and the relationships between men and women, men and men, women and women, change in society. Thus, while it is true that women were subordinated to men before capitalism and that this has affected the position of women in capitalist society, it is also true that the context of oppression we fight against now is specific to a society in which the capacity of human beings to create is appropriated by privately owned capital and in which the things produced are exchanged as commodities. Part 2 of this book is about the peculiar nature of female production in advanced capitalism, and about the part that the sexual division of labour and the family play in maintaining commodity production.

Rather than opposing *existing* relations within the family, or the *existing* consciousness of women under capitalism to relations in commodity production and the dominant consciousness in society, which is white, male, and ruling class, we have to examine the particular nature of the immediate antagonisms and contradictory tendencies generated by capital as it seeks its own self-expansion. Capitalism distorts the way in which human beings can reproduce themselves and the means of life. It makes free creation impossible in every aspect of life. But it also lays the basis for control over areas of life the organization of which were previously regarded as outside human power. Potentially, human procreation can now be controlled by human beings, just as work could be organized and owned by the workers themselves. We are beginning to understand how we reproduce ourselves through our relations with others and the world in which we find ourselves. The dangers are evident, but so, too, are the possibilities.

An understanding of the way women reproduce the forces of production and their own lives in capitalism is integral to an understanding of the exploitation of the wage-labourer. It seems to me that such an understanding will be a collective task, not the work of any one individual. Part 2 is far from being a total explanation or description of what happens to women in capitalism. It is a sketch and some bits are sketched in more carefully than others. The particular aspects of life I describe seem gloomy and pessimistic because I have tried to sketch the anatomy of oppression rather than to present a complete picture of life as it is lived. In real life we are happy, we love, and play, but *despite* the conditions in which we can become persons. The point is to change those conditions, not to make a virtue out of small personal triumphs over adversity.

In fact, behind this book there is a basic optimism. I think we are at the beginning of new social and personal possibilities, both for women and for men. Just as the making of the working class in the early stages of capitalism brought the promise – still not realized – of control over the conditions of human production, and thus the end of class, so the women's revolt in advanced capitalism brings a new hope. By giving expression to the hitherto silent frustrations of women who spend their lives in unrecognized labour in the home, who are helpless in pregnancy and childbirth without a man, who carry subordination within their souls from the earliest memory of childhood, this revolt has unleashed a new species of social passion. The articulation and exploration of the nature and source of that passion, which comes from the social situation of women now, through a movement, makes a new understanding of how to resist capitalism practicable.

Early liberal, equal-rights feminism tended to imagine that there could be changes in woman's position in capitalism without either transforming the outer world of production or the inner world of the family and sexuality. Although these problems were raised by women in the revolutionary movement in the twenties, the Marxist tradition, as feminism declined in the late thirties, increasingly emphasized the economic improvements of woman's position at work and the changes in legal relations. Important as these changes were, they obscured the ideological role of the family in maintaining capitalism and also led Marxists completely to ignore the nature of female production in the family. The new feminism of women's liberation has forced examination of these questions. At first, like the black movement, women became aware of the tip of the iceberg, the culture and consciousness of capitalist society. The distortion in the Marxist tradition which tended to identify the material world only with the conditions of commodity production and the social relations which come directly from work on the cash-nexus, held back understanding of the interaction between commodity production and other aspects of life under capitalism. The family and school are the most obvious examples. Marxist theory has thus continually lagged behind the new forms of organization, that of women, of gays, and of students. These new organizational forms have been the result of developments within capitalism.

Capitalism does not only exploit the wage-earner at work, it takes from men and women the capacity to develop their potential fully in every area of life. It twists the lives not only of those who are directly involved in production, but the lives of those who are for some reason or other excluded from producing commodities: children, old people and the ill, as well as women. Women as a group span both the world of commodity production, and production and reproduction in the home. In their own lives the two coexist painfully. Traditionally, the interior, private world of the home is feminine and thus the integration of women into the public world of work and industry is only partial. The contradiction which appears clearly in capitalism between family and industry, private and public, personal and impersonal, is the fissure in women's consciousness through which revolt erupts. The clash between the mass scale of commodity production and the micro-unit of the family and intimate sexual fantasy is thus the moment of women's liberation. But the questions which come out of women's liberation are of significance not only for women. How can we mobilize the resistance of many different sections of society? How can we bring together in our practice the separations in ourselves which paralyse us? How can we connect to our everyday living the abstract commitment to make a society without exploitation and oppression? What is the relationship between the objective changes in capitalism and our new perceptions of social revolution? What are the ways in which we can organize together without sacrificing our autonomy?

I consider the solution to exploitation and oppression to be communism, despite the hollow resonance the word has acquired. It seems to me that the cultural and economic liberation of women is inseparable from the creation of a society in which all people no longer have their lives stolen from them, and in which the conditions of their production and reproduction will no longer be distorted or held back by the subordination of sex, race, and class.

PART 1

Through the Looking-Glass

They have learnt to examine how capitalism is oppressing them ... it helps them to understand the relationship between their struggles and the struggles of other groups in our society. The deepest awareness of the evils of the capitalist system and the most unshakeable commitment to overthrowing that system is attained, not by studying socialist classics nor by working for someone else's 'cause', but by people examining the features of their own specific oppression. Women learnt not to wait for liberation to be won for them by radical (white) males, but to create their own issues and do it themselves. In the process of destroying the 'myth of inactivity' they are not only developing their own potentials as revolutionaries, but the movement itself will contribute to the struggle against capitalism.

Gill Simms, *I.S. Women's Newsletter*, no. 4.

the guiding thread: no
generalizations about man or woman
any distinctions are: irrelevant,
the choice merely between images

at least, that's what it thought
until a beastie glared back from
the mirror; and suddenly
back from the cradle jumped

the giant and Baba Yaya
in her three-legged chicken hut

and the pike who always got the perch

it all shudders so furiously
that no hand can steady it

for fear momentum
will disrupt the fingers
tiny tiny
            pieces of glass
jagging in different parts
of the planet; jeering, but there's
no blood

she did suffer, the witch;
trying to peer round the looking
glass, she forgot
someone was in the way.

Michelene, 'Reflexion',
Shrew, May 1971

CHAPTER 1

The Problem without a Name

Just what was this problem that has no name? What were the words women used when they tried to express it? Sometimes a woman would say "I feel empty somehow ... incomplete." Or she would say "I feel as if I don't exist."

Betty Friedan,
The Feminine Mystique

Why did it take us so long to make a movement like women's liberation? To start with we had consciously to recognize our femaleness and see through the existing versions of femininity which surrounded us. This was very difficult. There were distorting mirrors everywhere. People like me who were 17 in 1960 inherited a political feminist hiatus. Throughout the previous decade it had been as if there were no longer any reason to complain. Women were taught to regard themselves as satisfied. There was an enormous barrage of propaganda which served to create what Betty Friedan called 'the feminine mystique'. Dissatisfaction must be a personal failure. They faced their own experience completely alone. This made it very difficult for women to write about liberation in this period without having first to prove that there wasn't something wrong with them. Inevitably this restricted how far they could think. This was of course related to the general political climate of the cold war which made any form of radical activity difficult and lonely. But it was also because on the surface it looked as if women in the western capitalist countries were quite happy with things as they were. The tone of things was very much 'We're sitting pretty thank you'. The fifties was an era of elaborate hair-dos, constraining clothes and Dr Spock. Letters appeared in the papers from women saying they didn't want to have careers. The child psychologists stressed breast-feeding. Women with husbands who had been in the war went through paroxysms of guilt at the thought of leaving their small children. The bogy of mother deprivation was let loose.[1] The nurseries closed up. Immediately after the war women had left the skilled jobs they had had in the factories. Draughtswomen became housewives. Pastel colours were everywhere. In England the young queen and her family reinforced the idyll of love and marriage. Women were soon reabsorbed back into industry doing women's work. But the guilt about working mothers and latch-key children persisted. Propaganda for domestic bliss did not only come from the right. 'Left-wing' sociologists stood firm on the sanctity of the family.

The communist and Trotskyist movements retained theoretical commitment to the emancipation of women. But it was phrased in terms of the need to involve women in production and it was in a language which could not really express the feelings of women in post-war capitalism. Similarly the tone of the kind of feminism which had survived the movement for the vote, with its gritty get-in-and-at-them note was somehow off-key. The good-brick kind of girl like Katharine Hepburn in *The Rainmaker* was being superseded by the sexual-little-girl-lost-who-gets-the-nice-feller-with-glasses-who-conveniently-happens-to-be-a-millionaire. When people talked about equal rights there was a curious feeling that the record had stuck somewhere.

Betty Friedan's *The Feminine Mystique* came out of this period. It must have been a very difficult book to write because she started by pursuing an apparently completely submerged discontent. She graphically describes a sense of isolation. The atmosphere is of a suburban coffee meeting in an American city at the end of the decade. You can almost hear the chink of the cups on the saucers, and the slight brushing of stockinged legs

1. For a fuller discussion of this see Lee Comer, *The Myth of Motherhood*, Spokesman Pamphlet no. 21, Nottingham.

as they cross and uncross with the restrained restlessness of women who have been reasonable and nice all their lives.

The problem lay buried, unspoken for many years in the minds of American women. It was a strange stirring, a sense of dissatisfaction, a yearning that women suffered in the middle of the twentieth century in the United States. Each suburban wife struggled with it alone. As she made the beds, shopped for groceries, matched slip cover material, ate peanut butter sandwiches, chauffeured Cub Scouts and Brownies, lay beside her husband at night, she was afraid to ask even of herself the silent question: 'Is this all?' [2]

Betty Friedan calls it 'the problem that has no name'[3] because it did not fit into the same categories as the problems which had already been given names when she was writing. These women were not economically exploited, they did not sell their labour power, they were not hard up. They did not lack *things*. On the contrary, they often had too many things. But they felt that their lives were empty. They did not know who they were or what they wanted to become. It was by no means apparent that their situation could be understood politically. How could you organize round a sense of emptiness? In fact the strength of the book comes from the dauntless way in which she unravels and tracks down the origins of the mystique before any political implications were apparent. She uncovers the shift in women's magazine stories, the uses of popular anthropology and psychology, the changing emphasis in higher education, early marriages, anxiety about sexual performance. Her book was a revelation to many women because it was so determinedly about everyday matters. And most of our lives are 'everyday'. It included all those little things which became so important because women encountered them over and over again.

The weakness of the book was its remedies. She sees more and better education as the answer; there is vague reference to a 'new life plan' and the glimpse of a movement, but it's a movement which can only see itself shuffling about within capitalism. She excludes working-class women from the terms of reference and never penetrates the manifestations of women's oppression

2. Betty Friedan, *The Feminine Mystique*, Penguin, London 1968, p. 13.
3. ibid., p. 17.

through to the material structure of society, so the 'feminine mystique' retains its mystery. But she still peeled off important layers of confusion.

In the chapter on 'The Functional Freeze, The Feminine Protest, and Margaret Mead' she describes how Margaret Mead's extremely popular anthropological work tended to be used to justify the perpetuation of existing male and female 'roles'. The vision of bare-breasted women in the South Seas 'where a woman succeeds and is envied by man just by being a woman' was tempting to American women struggling off to work in the rush hour. The romance of being a career girl began to wear thin. The gloss of small-town girl makes good in big city only just concealed the real exploitation of female white-collar workers. Behind the enthusiasm for discovering a distinct role and the natural-childbirth breast-feeding movement was undoubtedly a dissatisfaction with life in a modern capitalist society. But as Betty Friedan points out it assumed a most reactionary form. 'The yearning is for a return to the Garden of Eden: a garden where woman need only forget the divine discontent born of education to return to a world in which male achievement becomes merely a poor substitute for child-bearing.'[4]

The reasoning went like this. The function of women in our society is to reproduce. Our system of higher education operates in contradiction to this, and thus creates a situation of imbalance which makes women unhappy. Feminism is the product of this frustration. If we were to educate women to fulfil their role as reproducers all would be well. This was handy reasoning with a female labour force that had to be sent home or taught its place doing women's work at low pay. It was useful stuff to all manner of gentlemen in high places paid large sums to devise educational reports to enable young women to keep tight budgets and cook good dinners. It was ignored that it was rather naïve to expect women to fulfil some abstracted 'natural' function in a most unnatural society particularly when contraceptives were reducing the time women were spending in childbirth. There were apparently no prospects either for the women who were already educated. Their aspirations were not considered to be important. The

4. Betty Friedan, *The Feminine Mystique*, Penguin, London 1968, p. 125.

idea of female 'roles' served to give a spurious modernity to an old conservatism. Just as the eighteenth-century bishops had fulminated against the idea of working-class education because it conflicted with the notion of station and their own class interest, which needed the 'hewers of wood' in their place, social science contributed towards a notion of femininity in which baby-doll became a new natural-savage substitute. As it became less and less possible politically to sentimentalize workers, blacks, or the colonized as representatives of the primitive, the yearning of the bourgeois for animality which did not shatter the repression and work-discipline essential to capitalism focused completely on women.[5]

Ironically all this was completely at variance with Margaret Mead's own life and work. She and her friend and close colleague Ruth Benedict were intellectual pioneers in anthropology when it was very unusual for women to study the subject. Both of them were emphatic on the need for both sexes to develop their full potential. But they reacted against the tendency in feminism which refused to admit and examine the actual difference between men and women. They both believed that by accumulating more data on women they would be able to throw light on what were essential aspects of femininity rather than forcing women into a masculine mould. Ruth Benedict wrote in her journal in the early 1920s, 'The emotional part of woman's life – that part which makes her a woman – must be brought out of the dark and allowed to put forth its best.'[6] She wanted the 'thorough-going differences between men and women', which were 'both deeper in some respects and shallower in others than are today generally recognized', to be carefully studied. She believed external changes were necessary, but that 'the ultimate objective remains an inward affair, a matter of attitude.'[7] Later she wrote about her inability to realize her sense of personal experience, 'that sees existence

5. These ideas are still alive and well. Go and see *Easy Rider* again, or read Edmund Leach, *Culture and Nature or 'La Femme Sauvage'*, The Stevenson Lecture, Bedford College, 1969.

6. Margaret Mead, *Writings of Ruth Benedict – An Anthropologist at Work*, Cambridge, Mass., 1959, p. 147.

7. ibid., p. 146.

under the form of eternity . . . that fire upon our flesh shall burn as a knife that cuts to the bone, and joy strip us like a naked blade'[8] in the external world of work and obligation. Even when she was satisfied with her work, 'It's always busy work I do with my left hand, and part of me watches grudging the waste of life time.' It was not evident to her that the aim of life should be activity. She wished she had been born in a time when contemplation was the end of life. But both this sense of dislocation with the inner and outer world and the commitment to the growth of the specific nature of women were eclipsed. In the 1960s Margaret Mead was left wondering about the 'retreat into fecundity'.[9] It was evident that the mere existence of social data was not enough to reveal what a woman was. The political force of the need to keep women within the 'role' capitalism had assigned to them was sufficiently strong to turn any discoveries about the position of women in completely different cultures into a justification for the existing structure of sexual relationships.

The notion of female destiny which came from anthropology combined with the 'anatomic destiny' of a vulgarized Freudianism to make the distinction between anatomic and cultural possibility even harder to disentagle. Freud's own rather odd ideas about female sexuality assumed a religious quality in the hands of his followers. They were apparently not unrelated to his personal attitudes. Betty Friedan quotes a letter he wrote in 1883 criticizing J. S. Mill which was reactionary within its own time. 'If I imagined my gentle sweet girl as a competitor, it would only end in my telling her, as I did seventeen months ago, that I am fond of her and that I implore her to withdraw from the strife into the calm, uncompetitive activity of my home.'[10]

He recognized that different upbringings would equip women to go into the outside world men had made but that this would destroy the most 'delightful thing the world can offer us – our ideal of womanhood'. It didn't occur to him to criticize the economic basis of competitive capitalism. Despite his cautious conservatism in a complicated and self-doubting way he realized

8. Margaret Mead, *Writings of Ruth Benedict – An Anthropologist at Work*, Cambridge, Mass., 1959, pp. 154–5.

9. Quoted in Friedan, *The Feminine Mystique*, p. 130.

10. ibid., p. 98.

from his researches in the nineties into the prevalent hysteria of Viennese upper-class women the supreme importance of sexuality in the lives both of men and women. He repeatedly stressed the tragic implication for human beings of thwarted sexuality and pointed out how women especially were doomed frequently to unhappiness simply because of inadequate contraceptive measures. These were radical and liberating discoveries at the time. However, later, though he was critical about the use of 'masculine' and 'feminine' as scientific terms, he made extremely loaded statements based on inadequate evidence which were accepted subsequently. His main ideas about female psychology were developed when he was already ill from cancer and could not test them with case history material. He was not unaware of this himself. 'In his last years Freud stated with increasing frequency the significance of the gaps and obscurities in his own theories: one that preoccupied him was the meaning of being a woman, the nature of femininity. Simply what is it? "I cannot discover what it is, to be feminine." '[11]

His preoccupation with the question was important but unfortunately it has only been spasmodically followed up by attempts to distinguish between biology, psychology and history.[12] In the case of women all three still remain in considerable obscurity.

11. Juliet Mitchell, 'Why Freud?', *Shrew*, December 1970, p. 23, and *Woman's Estate*, Penguin, 1971. (This section is based on her *Shrew* article.)

12. See generally:

Norman O. Brown, *Life Against Death*, Sphere, 1968.

H. Marcuse, *Eros and Civilization*, Allen Lane The Penguin Press, 1969.

Reimut Reiche, *Sexuality and Class Struggle*, New Left Books, 1970.

On women's liberation in particular:

Betty Friedan, 'The Sexual Solipsism of Sigmund Freud', in *The Feminine Mystique*, op. cit.

Naomi Weinstein, *Kinde, Küche, Kirche: Psychology Constructs the Female*, New England Free Press pamphlet, and Agitprop, London.

Anne Koedt, *The Myth of the Vaginal Orgasm*, New England Free Press pamphlet, and Women's Liberation Workshop, London.

Eva Figes, *Patriarchal Attitudes*, Faber & Faber, 1970.

Shulamith Firestone, *The Dialectic of Sex: The Case for Feminist Revolution*, Jonathan Cape, 1971.

Germaine Greer, *The Female Eunuch*, Paladin, 1971.

Juliet Mitchell, *Woman's Estate*, Penguin, 1971.

The psychoanalytic work of Karen Horney is particularly valuable for this reason. Karen Horney studied psychoanalyis in Berlin before the First World War. Both the political climate of Berlin after the war and less deterministic ideas of science meant that she was inclined to stress the need to account for the effects of the environment as well as the internal psychological state of the patient. Later when she went to America to escape the rise of fascism in Germany she became familiar with anthropological work and ideas of cultural relativism. As early as 1922 in a paper 'On the Genesis of the Castration Complex in Women' she criticized Freud's claim that penis envy alone was responsible for female castration fantasies. Later she went on to challenge other Freudian theories with a combination of her own social perspective and clinical findings. For example, in her paper 'The Denial of the Vagina' in 1933 she pointed out that her male patients showed desire for female sexual characteristics. In *The Neurotic Personality of Our Time*, published after she left Germany, she used Ruth Benedict's *Patterns of Culture* to criticize Freud's tendency to make generalizations about human nature without recognizing that he spoke from a particular sexual and cultural point of view.

But it was the extraordinary achievement of *The Second Sex*, published in France in 1949, which first attempted a total synthesis of the biological, psychological, cultural and historical destiny of the concept and situation of women. Simone de Beauvoir engaged with the 'mystique' of femininity but she did not neglect new evidence which was available to her from work in psychology and anthropology. She tackled also a philosophical tendency implicit in rationalism which had passed over into both the liberal feminist and Marxist approaches to emancipation. This was the way in which women were seen as 'merely human beings arbitrarily designated by the word woman'.[13] The general cover of human-beingness camouflaged both the anatomical differences between men and women and concealed the manner in

13. Simone de Beauvoir, *The Nature of the Second Sex*, Four Square, 1968. (This work was originally published in French in one volume, but was translated into English as two volumes: *The Nature of the Second Sex* and *The Second Sex*.)

which the notion of the human being is male-defined in all forms of existing social organization – including the revolutionary party. In fact this defensive denial of actual difference left the way wide open for a crude and mechanical reduction of feminine potential to the body. It was easy for the anti-feminists to determine a woman by her anatomy because the feminists persisted in ignoring that her anatomy existed at all. It was thus not possible to go on and argue that both men and women were products both of anatomy and of history. Anatomic destiny was falsely extracted out of history or *vice versa.* By starting the task of disentangling femaleness from femininity Simone de Beauvoir indicated a new and transformed possibility – the movement from passivity into freedom.

The limitations in *The Second Sex* are limitations of its era. Simone de Beauvoir's presence in the book is somewhat aloof and impersonal, and many of the ideas are presented in an abstract way. In isolation, with no organized revolutionary feminist movement, the connection between feminism and revolution is necessarily laboured and abstract. Similarly the drying-up of Marxism during Stalin's rule made any attempt to introduce new areas of human consciousness difficult. There is thus a separation in *The Second Sex* between what de Beauvoir described in *Force of Circumstance* as a 'struggle of consciences' and the analysis of women's oppression in terms of the ownership of property. It was impossible for her at the time of writing to envisage a new active social consciousness of women.[14]

14. See Simone de Beauvoir, 'Today I've changed – I've really become a feminist', *Seven Days*, 8 March 1972, and Mitchell, *Woman's Estate*, pp. 81–2.

CHAPTER 2

Living Doll

I got myself a sleeping, walking, crying, talking Living Doll.

Cliff Richard, 'Living Doll', 1959.

When I was seventeen feminism meant to me shadowy figures in long old-fashioned clothes who were somehow connected with headmistresses who said you shouldn't wear high heels and make-up. It was all very prim and stiff and mainly concerned with keeping you away from boys. From dim childhood memories I had a stereotype of emancipated women: frightening people in tweed suits and horn-rimmed glasses with stern buns at the backs of their heads. Feminism was completely asexual. It didn't occur to me that it was anything to do with the double standard of sexual morality which hurt and humiliated me. Feminism seemed the very antithesis of the freedom I connected with getting away from home and school. When I saw myself able to live as I wanted I didn't have any specific idea of myself as a woman doing whatever I would be doing. I would simply be doing things. I didn't have any way of connecting myself politically and socially to a condition of womanhood. My recognition of women as a group was as creatures sunk into the very deadening circumstances from which I was determined to escape.

Most older women seemed like this to me. They seemed always to want to damp you down and hold you in. The few I knew who weren't like this, mainly my mother and my history teacher, I wanted to be as much like as possible. I had also collected a rag-bag of ideal women, in Mary Wollstonecraft, Olive Schreiner, Simone de Beauvoir, Doris Lessing. But none of them seemed either to have lives which remotely resembled mine, or to have quite the same problems that I encountered. On the other hand the 'mystique' was very much part of my life. There was pop music for example. My own sense of myself as a person directly conflicted with the kind of girl who was sung about in pop songs. When I was sixteen I remember feeling really angry about 'Living Doll' because it contradicted all the thoughtful proud bits of me. It cut away from all my inside efforts towards any identity. It hurt me particularly because when I tried to argue about it with a boy I really liked I felt terribly constrained by his contempt when he said that was how he liked girls.

Later I defended myself implicitly by distinguishing myself in my head from other girls who seemed to accept their fate without resistance. It was easy to develop this sense of separateness because most of the people I was at school with left to go on typing courses. They all became much more smart and confident than those of us who stayed on. I consoled myself by retreating into an intellectual inner world of mysticism and reverie; I read anything and everything I could find which would help me build an important little private sphere of 'culture'. By an intensely theoretical route I acquired wild and dangerous notions about sex and marriage which were in marked contrast both to what everyone around me thought and to my own total ignorance in practice. I could never think quickly enough somehow to translate the gametes and zygotes we learned about in biology into information about what *Honey* called 'how far to go'. So I would quickly abdicate my theoretical position and say 'no' on the rare occasions in which physical circumstances made 'yes' possible. I kicked myself for my cowardice every time and was far too much of a puritan to bear the gulf between theory and practice comfortably.

The sources of my notions about sexual liberation were bizarre and diversified. Shaw's prefaces, Ibsen's plays, a paperback version of Havelock Ellis, a biography of him which dwelt on the significance of his mother urinating, and inevitably Lawrence and Miller. I struggled through guilt and silence with these and they gave me courage to resist being called a slut. But I realized that the fact that I could use this 'culture' to defend myself was a mere chance. After I left school and was hitching through France chalking on the pavements before de Gaulle made it difficult to get money like this, I met girls who had no such protection. I admired them because they seemed able to face contempt better than I could without any false coverings.

I was lucky enough to fall in love with an art-student who I found very awe-inspiring because he was working-class, an anarchist and smoked pot, and came from a mysterious world of Soho coffee bars. He vanished very quickly but not before he'd told me you had to be on the side of the workers, and to see beauty in the bottom of coffee cups, that Bakunin said revolutionaries shouldn't get hung up on love, and that Wilhelm Reich had said everything that needed to be said about sex. He was the first man I'd ever met who knew about the things I wanted to know. As he went away so quickly I was left to find them out on my own. This was difficult. Trying to read Reich in Leeds in 1961 was still more or less impossible if you didn't have a large academic 'psychology' label on you which proved you weren't a dirty-minded person. I wish I had managed to – it would perhaps have saved me a lot of time. Instead I acquired an implicit way of thinking which made it impossible for me to see my own situation in terms of social and historical change. Things just happened for and in themselves. I picked up an insistence on direct experience and feeling. I was inordinately suspicious of reason and analysis. Only moments of intense subjectivity seemed to have any honesty or authenticity. All removed ways of thinking appeared to me as necessarily suspect. Intellectually this came from strong doses of Camus, Colin Wilson, Nathaniel West, and Sartre's *Nausea*. But emotionally it was reinforced by rock music, the beat movement and a dislike of upper-class arty people who had opinions on everything. Every rock record simply was. The words were subordinate to the rhythm and the music went straight to your cunt and hit the bottom of your spine. They were like a great release after all the super-consolation romantic ballads like 'Three Coins in a Fountain', 'Love is a Many Splendoured Thing', or the twee coyness of 'Love and Marriage'. Its cultural impact continued long after rock 'n roll faded out. The atmosphere of rock comes through *Howl* and *On the Road*. There is the same sense of release, the same explosion of pent-upness. I managed to get *On the Road* as a school prize because we were allowed to choose what we wanted. It was a hardback copy and the cover had 'Drugs, liquor, girls' written all over it. The categories didn't trouble me at all. I simply switched sex as I did with Miller and Lawrence and identified with the men because they were exciting and adventurous. *On the Road* was 'a coded message of discontent',[1] an exultation of moving on. Hitch-hiking was made to seem infinitely exciting. The fact that the girls invariably got a rough ride in the beat movement never really dawned on me until later. I just thought it was somehow inevitable that girls were meant to be heroically tough and miraculously soft at the same time. Exhaustingly I tried to live the contradiction.

The image I had of the ultimate man didn't help much. He was a mixture of James Dean and Marlon Brando and immensely mobile. The ultimate man was a light traveller, an early ancestor of Peter Fonda in *Easy Rider*. He rarely spoke about philosophic matters but simply grunted his profound and intense version of the world and so communicated honestly because he didn't mess about with words. He defined his existence through a twitch of his nose or the flicker of his eye. He was constantly leaving and arriving, he rode a bike, hitched, rode on the top of trains, or stowed away. He ate magic mushrooms on mountains in Mexico, or crossed the Sahara four times at least. He was the kind of man who wouldn't tie you down because he had nothing spare to cover you with. He was a man who had holes in his pants and holes in T shirts, and holes in his jeans, and holes in his sweater but the biggest hole of all was in his heart. Hearts, as far as I was concerned, were expendable. A man with a heart seemed a soppy sort of man. He belonged to the slushy pop songs and was nothing to do with me. My fantasy of the ultimate man was in fact extremely religious. I wanted a new kind of saint. I puzzled patiently over Norman Mailer's *The White Negro*, which I found in a paperback called *Protest* in a little shop in a Yorkshire seaside town. Most of it I didn't understand at first but some phrases stuck in my head.

1. David Widgery, 'Goodbye Jack Kerouac', *Oz*, November 1970.

> The real argument which the mystic must always advance is the very intensity of his private vision – his argument depends from the vision precisely because what was felt in the vision is so extraordinary that no rational argument, no hypothesis of 'oceanic feelings' and certainly no sceptical reductions can explain away what has become for him the reality more real than the reality of closely reasoned logic.[2]

This was the only place I could find an explicit statement of what I felt to be 'real'. Instead of the proverbial prince who came in fairy stories if you waited long enough and managed to be beautiful, I hoped quietly for some friendly psychopath to notice that under my remarkably healthy exterior I was in fact suitably intense and fraught for the most extended and crazed imagination.

Politically the immediate implications of this way of seeing were extremely reactionary. If things just happened they were going to happen anyway and it was pointless trying to make or stop them. You couldn't sit down and plot a strategy because only immediate sensation was valid. The sexual liberation of Lawrence and Miller was one in which women were projections of male notions of the man's sexual freedom. My male stereotype was an elaborate romanticization of a person who was so self-centred it was impossible for me to get dependent on him. But emotionally it all acted like a vacuum cleaner. I dumped out my inheritance of pastel colours and princes and collected a new bag of black sweaters, jeans, psychopaths and beat fantasy. I finally discarded them like a lot of absentminded clutter and clambered off onto a completely new way of seeing.

New Journey

In complete contradiction to myself I kept wanting to get back to the beginning. I wanted to find out how things happened and why. I kept on trying to trace all phenomena to their source. I wanted to be in on the birth of everything – poke my nose into the mystery of things. So even when half of me refused to let

2. Norman Mailer, 'The White Negro', now in *Advertisements for Myself*, Deutsch, 1961, p. 286.

myself go off, half of me kept starting on great expeditions. Sometimes I sailed off heroically into the future on a big red double-decker. Mainly though I crawled through the undergrowth with a tiny ball of string tied to the branch of a tree so I'd be able to get back to where I'd started from. I never did of course, but even the intention was enough. It really wasn't possible at once to situate myself, distinguish the shapes of things, put names to them, distil them, watch them change, and live totally in every moment innocent of the passing of time and events.

In my first year at university it slowly became evident to me that intense visionary moments didn't help you to read Gibbon and Macaulay or study the growth of the judiciary in the Middle Ages or the boundaries of the Austro-Hungarian empire. I found this kind of history boring at the best of times. But my commitment to my own preoccupations tended to make it the worst of times. I stayed in a kind of abeyance for a year, surfacing into some interest in history at rare moments. When I was nineteen and in my second year a combination of things made me change. I met a man who loved me patiently until I had orgasms and who resolutely bullied me into Marxism. Mine was a timely but painful conversion. He was much better at arguing logically than I was and I burst into tears every time I was defeated.

But a sense of the reality of class came from my deeply class-conscious background. My father was an engineering salesman who had worked his way up and was proud of it, and class distinctions in northern industrial towns are sharp and clearly delineated. It meant that I could understand when Marxists said my beatniking was escapism. Marx seemed to me to write about the past in a way which I had always wanted to discover it. Things welded into shape and then exploded. I started particularly to read about the history of the socialist and anarchist movements, trying to find how he fitted in. I made Emma Goldman my heroine. I admired her for fighting as a woman but I still made no feminist connections. A friend of mine called Judith was always talking about Simone de Beauvoir and getting women into the students' union. I hated the students' union; political people seemed to be just out to advance themselves. I didn't really understand why she was getting so worked up. My emancipation still seemed to me to be a matter of individual choice, though I was beginning to understand that the emancipation of the working class was not. Apart from odd meetings of Marxist groups, however, and marching off to the Regional Seat of Government at Reading, I had no notion of practical routine political activity.

I went in head first when I left university and went to live in London by joining my local Young Socialists. I had no idea what I was in for. I sat Friday in and Friday out in a puce-coloured Labour Party room in Hackney while innumerable species of 'Trots' hurled incomprehensible initials at each other in exclusive intercommunication which completely whizzed past my ears. Although they all knew each other incestuously well they addressed everyone very ceremoniously as 'the comrades in the tendency at the back (or the front)'. They prefaced every statement with 'The correct Marxist position is . . .' Accusations of bonapartism and petty bourgeois status abounded. They had their own peculiar terms for everything. Signs of insubordination like giggling were harangued from a great height. 'Certain comrades show an extremely cynical attitude.'

The 'tendencies' seemed to assume different clothes as outward and manifest signs of their distinctness. International Socialism – at that time quite a small group – were predominantly donkey-jacketed, while Militant – a deep-entrist lot – wore brown suedette jackets with fur collars. All kinds of other odds and sods blew in for particular meetings, but I didn't have enough time to work out their cultural peculiarities in any detail. There were innumerable small Irish Marxist groups, floating members of the Socialist Party of Great Britain, amicable but inconclusive visits from the Young Communist League, denunciatory ones from the Socialist Labour League.

I spent a lot of time watching how people reacted to each other and I became slowly versed in the intense if narrow rigours of Trotskyism between the collapse of CND and the rise of the student movement. Gradually I started to decode the initials and the terms. The main key was the Russian revolution. I was soon able to classify someone's 'tendency' in, at most, their three opening sentences. But it's hard to say what I learned directly. The speakers all had things called 'analyses' which they maintained were absolutely correct. The only way of arguing was to knock one analysis down with another. They came ready-made and you learned them by rote from pamphlets or articles. Their analyses were nicely all-embracing but I was always left with a sense of not knowing what had happened. Between conflicting correctnesses I thought there must be some connecting facts lurking somewhere.

Occasionally I exploded into anger when they penetrated some area of my own experience. Like the man from Militant who solemnly told everyone that drugs, drink and women were a capitalist plot to seduce the workers from Marxism. The irony of this was extreme because there had been a spate of pregnancies and the pub was a kind of Mecca. As we grappled together under the merciless neon lights, huddled in our coats in winter, wriggling on the tubular chairs, longing to get into the warmth and comfort of the pub, the mysteries of social change passed slowly in front of my nose. The dialectic rebounded from one corner to the other. I sat there in a bewildered kind of way for about three and a half years from 1964 to 1967 emerging sometimes to leaflet for a recruitment campaign, or to go to the odd outside meeting on the incomes policy, the founding meeting of the Vietnam Solidarity Campaign, meetings and demonstrations in support of the seamen on strike, or tenants' movements. I made some friends; the implications of my class background were drummed into me; my political perceptions grew out of a working-class-based local organization which was integrally bound to Marxism. Most important I encountered a Marxism in practice in which there was no single orthodoxy but much disputation. Now it makes some sense – then it made none. I remained bound to the group by the peculiar blend of guilt and masochism which builds up in such circumstances.

I learned from older Marxist friends that alternative Marxisms existed beyond and behind my world of the YS. They talked to me about the Communist Party, about Hungary, Algeria, about the Social Democratic Federation in Leeds. They connected politics to the way you lived. It seemed I was just part of a great ebbing and flowing mass of people, who fell in love, suffered, activated, died, but who all had to make conscious if tortured decisions which had a small but not insignificant effect. Most important, some of these people were women. The socialism I discovered from them was one which was explicitly committed to human dignity and which assumed that women should be as proud and responsible as men. Through them I relived a politics which I had never known and did not relate to my own immediate experience. The history of the working-class movement I was discovering for myself was another dimension of this.

Footholds

I had been going in one direction. I gradually became aware that I was missing pockets and crevices all along the way. My old 'things in themselves' feeling erupted again. The dislocation between my sense of my self inside and my behaviour outside was clear and undeniable. I felt I could never bring them together unless I re-entered myself. So I started to go into the world of personal experience that I had earlier half-discarded. This time I started a new kind of exploration, returning to the me who cried because I couldn't play bar football, who had periods and watched the sun sink, who longed to return to before puberty, splashing through puddles in the mud, who did headstands in the park before men bothered to look at your knickers. I was struck with the tragedy of the sexual divide and the way it had hobbled me. I went backwards and forwards to no place in particular. My hands became my father's and returned to the bone of death. My legs became my mother's, whose ankles grew fat like hers never did, and became like those of the old women I shrank from becoming when I saw them on the bus clutching shopping-bags to their breasts where once men's heads had lain. My own sense of myself as a woman turned outwards. I realized that the me who talked of socialism and class still wanted desperately to distinguish myself from the swollen legs of old women, from the white beaten-down faces of young women I met in the launderette. I defined my own survival and emergence despite them. In class terms I knew it was at their expense but this was not enough. I was distinguishing myself as a woman as much as a person from another class. My relationship to working-class men was quite different. I was distinguishing myself essentially as a woman. Slowly I began to move towards a perception of myself in relation to other women whom I had always seen as quite separate from me.

I had been picking up and putting down *The Second Sex* since I'd been at university. But I found the ideas very inaccessible at first. They were not easy to internalize. I couldn't relate them to myself. But in fact Simone de Beauvoir must have been seeping through my way of seeing everything. I had a long gap when I didn't read her, but I was getting at the things she said by a completely different route. I found myself uncomfortably straddled between the left and the underground, always arguing with both sides. I felt impatient with the hippies because they'd never recognized class, but impatient also with the left-wing people who'd never let themselves feel any of the things the underground found important.

I was aware of condescension and selfishness which often appeared thinly disguised as 'cool'. I watched this particularly when it was directed against girls I knew. The passivity of the ideal 'chick' – serene and spiritual although she was completely broke and standing in endless NAB queues, with a baby on her breast and her tarot cards on her knee – was transparently a new version of the old mystique.

But I also met girls who hadn't been educated and had no academic protections, who had got out of the working class by the only way open to them, who went off and danced in clubs, and shifted for themselves and were raddled for it. I met others who, calmly and quietly with their man on heroin, planned co-operative sewing schemes for pop groups and were moving towards their own kind of dignity, out of the point of being a 'chick'. They weren't like me. But they were enough like me in a different way for me to respect what they were doing.

At the same time I sensed something very complicated going on in the heads of men who were about my age. It's for them to write about this. I wish they would very soon. The most eloquent records exist in the songs we've been listening to since the sixties. In rock 'n roll the emotions were rather simple. Elvis was there – true, he had his chain around his neck as 'Your Teddy Bear', and he promised to come 'any way you want me', but it was a rather confident and voluntary submission. Then there was an interval of Italianate cleaned-up pop, in which the girls were girls and the boys were boys and they always met. With the Beatles the words of pop music became much more delicate and precise. Songs like 'Norwegian Wood' and 'Eleanor Rigby' communicated complicated feelings in a lyrical kind of way. The girls in their songs were all people, not just pop stereotypes, but still male-defined. This has meant that the image of women that comes through them is difficult to work out and react to. The Stones and Bob Dylan were often more explicitly nasty. They kept on saying that's how it is, in brief, ugly, short, and real, and the women who listened to them had better learn it. They left no space at the margins for any of the old security or decency or obligation. They grind right down to the bone. But even so their songs are really often very scared. It's as if they sense a threat to the old way of being a man, before women's liberation became a movement. Part of them wants really to crush the new ways in which women behave, both in bed and outside, but the other part of them goes out to women because they are against how most men put them down. I can understand this because I'm split in two in different parts of me. Their music attracts and threatens me. It is beautiful, but at my expense, and I am always external to the way they are thinking. It seemed as if Janis Joplin was fighting through to an answer. But she went through too much pain to get there safely.

In 1967 a strange thing occurred in London called 'The Dialectics of Liberation'. It was a peculiar collection of the incompatible and reluctant forces of liberation. The revolutionary left – or bits of it – encountered the mind-blowers. Having carried them both around inside me for some time I was anxious to see how they would meet. It was more of a two-week-long trauma than a conference. I experienced a severe sense of dislocation throughout. But I started to try and work out for myself the implications of what Stokeley Carmichael and the other black-power people were talking about. Their emotional rejection–attraction to white women forced me to think about myself and also labour at what the black women who sat silent still felt. The idea of taking hold of your own definitions stuck. So did the tortured delicacy of Laing. I began to use both ways of thinking for myself. In the same year Karen Horney's *Feminine Psychology* appeared rather quietly and obscurely. I was fascinated by it because she described areas of experience I had never seen written down, but I hooked a lifetime of experiences suddenly onto her clear statement of male cultural hegemony. Just as Marxism had made sense because it made the experience of class suddenly something you could understand and describe historically, so my sexual situation became socially comprehensible.

General political developments were making it impossible to sit back and watch any more. A class of Port of London Authority messenger boys at a College of Further Education in East London greeted me with fascist 'Hail Enoch' salutes in '68 and they weren't joking. I saw the dockers demonstrating for Powell, and some men spat at me when I gave them leaflets. Flowers and love were a bit of a luxury now. At the same time the Vietnam campaign, the impact of May '68, the international student movement, and my connection with a paper called *Black Dwarf* meant a rush of political activity. But more than that it meant a new kind of political movement. The atmosphere around '68 was very much one in which culture and consciousness were emphasized at the expense of the objective circumstances in which we found ourselves. Despite the dangers of this it meant that all kinds of questions which had been forced out of Marxism when there were only the small groups to keep it alive came in again. In England the slowly accumulating influence of the old new left was very important, but also people branched out into unexplored territories. The rediscovery of our early perception of ourselves and our own sexuality entered politics – not as a theoretical question but as a passionate and practical demand scrawled on a bog wall in a sit-in. 'Give me back my past, my childhood, my body, my life.' This helped us to connect a sense of femaleness to our sense of ourselves as political animals. Our bodies at least were female.

When people talked about the effect of relations of domination in schools and universities on a micro-level it seemed reasonable to think about the family in the same way. Reich and Laing did after all. Again we were taken back to our femaleness. What tended to happen in fact, however, was that the emphasis in revolutionary culture was thwarted just as it awakened, because the culture which was presented as 'revolutionary' was so blatantly phallic. The masculine orientation had always been there but in a concealed form of respect for various Marxist authorities. The revolutionaries of '68 tore off the respect and stripped the authorities. Street-fighting man – the cult of Che, the paraphernalia of helmets, the militancy that could shout loudest – went around with naked genitals. He made his own self-assertion the biggest authority of all in the very moments he denounced the authoritarianism of the stolid, determinedly unemotional politics of the sects.

This contradiction was powerful enough to bring women like me in the revolutionary movement to a recognition of ourselves as women. At the time none of us had a clear idea of what was happening because we supported many of the feelings of '68 ourselves. I found myself in conflict in an increasing number of particular incidents, sexual banter, the whistling when women spoke, the way in which men divided us into two, either as comrades or as women they fucked. Once a man told me to stop being so 'effeminate'. There was an argument about putting pin-ups in the *Black Dwarf*. I began to talk to other women. We all seemed suddenly to be feeling similar things.

At the same time I was going over and over the same problems – how was it possible to relate my particular experiences as a woman to the Marxism I had inherited. How could I understand the manner in which society communicated itself through to the individual consciousness? How does individual consciousness translate itself back into a social movement? I felt personal experience outside the factory must relate to the Marxist discussion of consciousness which seemed to presume 'we are born at the age when we earn our first wages',[3] but I didn't see how. What were the implications of organizing around a sense of oppression rather

3. J.-P. Sartre, *Problem of Method*, Methuen, 1964, p. 62.

than simply around the means of production? Finally it seemed increasingly evident that it was impossible for revolutionary movements to survive in opposition to capitalism unless they consciously created their own culture which served to defend us all from the continual erosion of capitalism's version of the world and enabled us to project alternative values without being overwhelmed. But I did not understand how this could be done without making either mirrors of our immediate alienation or perpetually creating small, self-defeating, totalizing utopias which served only to exhaust everybody more by trying to live up to an impossibly ideal standard. I found some of these questions in Fanon, Reich, Sartre and Gramsci. But when women's liberation burst about my ears I suddenly saw ideas which had been roaming hopelessly round my head coming out in the shape of other people – women-people. Once again I started to find my bearings all over again. But this time we were going through the looking-glass together.

CHAPTER 3

Through the Looking-Glass

Life is not determined by consciousness but consciousness by life ... The individuals composing the ruling class possess among other things consciousness, and therefore think.

Karl Marx, *German Ideology*

Though she felt as a woman [Divine] thought as a 'man' ... And all the woman judgements she made were, in reality, poetical conclusions ... She does not wish to become a woman completely since she loathes women. She wants to be a man-woman: a woman when she is passive, a man when she acts. Thus this language relates her to an absence.

J.-P. Sartre, *Saint Genet*

I'll be your mirror, reflect what you are ...

Velvet Underground, 'I'll be Your Mirror'

Mirrors

When I was a little girl I was fascinated by the kind of dressing-table mirror which was in three parts. You could move the outer folding mirrors inwards and if you pressed your nose to the glass you saw reflections of yourself with a squashed nose repeated over and over again. I used to wonder which bit was really me. Where was I in all these broken bits of reflection? The more I tried to grasp the totality, the more I concentrated on capturing myself in my own image, the less I felt I knew who I was. The mirror held a certain magic. The picture started to assume its own reality. My sense of self-ness came back through the shape of my nose. I defined my own possibility in relation to the face I saw in front of me. But impatient with the inability of the image to act independently I used to want to walk through the mirror. I had a nagging and irreconcilable notion that if I could only get through the mirror a separate self would emerge who would confirm the existence of the first self by recognizing it. Without this recognition I felt invisible inside myself although my appearance was clearly visible in the glass. Sometimes in the effort to relate my internal bewilderment to the external phenomena of my self I would even peer round the back to see if anything changed round there. Of course it was always frustratingly the same. Just old brown unpolished wood which slightly grazed the tips of your fingers when you touched it. I thought I had finally found the secret in my mother's hand mirror which had glass on both sides. But that was no good either, just another illusion.

The vast mass of human beings have always been mainly invisible to themselves while a tiny minority have exhausted themselves in the isolation of observing their own reflections. Every mass political movement of the oppressed necessarily brings its own vision of itself into sight. At first this consciousness is fragmented and particular. The prevailing social order stands as a great and resplendent hall of mirrors. It owns and occupies the world as it is and the world as it is seen and heard. But the first glimpse of revolutionary possibility leaves a small but indestructible chink in its magnificent self-confidence. Capitalism now carries not chinks but great slits and gashes. It bears the mark of revolution.

In order to create an alternative an oppressed group must at once shatter the self-reflecting world which encircles it and, at the same time, project its own image onto history. In order to discover its own identity as distinct from that of the oppressor it has to become visible to itself. All revolutionary movements create their own ways of seeing. But this is a result of great labour. People who are without names, who do not know themselves, who have no culture, experience a kind of paralysis of consciousness. The first step is to connect and learn to trust one another.

Consciousness within the revolutionary movement can only become coherent and self-critical when its version of the world becomes clear not simply within itself but when it knows itself in relation to what it has created apart from itself. When we can look back at ourselves through our own cultural creations, our actions, our ideas, our pamphlets, our organization, our history, our theory, we begin to integrate a new reality. As we begin to know ourselves in a new relation to one another we can start to understand our movement in relation to the world outside. We can begin to use our self-consciousness strategically. We can see what we could not see before.

But there are many perils. Historical self-consciousness is a tumultuous and wayward odyssey which for many of us has only just begun. If mass revolutionary action has a relatively brief history, female revolutionary politics is a mere flicker in its midst. A new consciousness is a laborious thing. Now we are like babes thrashing around in darkness and unexplored space. The creation of an alternative world and an alternative culture cannot be the work of a day. But we cannot afford to waste time while reaction consolidates itself. Theoretical consistency is difficult – often it comes out as dogmatism. It is hard to steer any steady course while accepting that we will always aspire beyond what we can realize. It is hard to put out our hands and touch the past, harder still to bring the past into the future. Nor does the same definition necessarily do from one day to the next. Circumstances transform themselves and our relationship to them. Nothing seems fixed in the world. Familiar ideas don't fit the new reality. The mirror dissolves into a light show. When you watch a light show you see one coloured pattern created by the slides in a projector disintegrating in the very moment in which it appears distinctly and immediately to be altering its relationship to all the other colours which are themselves going through the same process according to their own unique pattern. Revolutionaries now have to accommodate themselves to organizing in the midst of a gigantic three-dimensional light show.

In all the movement and confusion there is a great darkness. Consciousness which comes from political action takes time to communicate itself. Connection is, at first, spasmodic and uncoordinated. It takes time to relate new and surprising versions of the world. We need to make a new reality through the action we take and through our organization in combination with one another. But we have to discover our own reality too or we will simply be subsumed. Solidarity has to be a collective consciousness which at once comes through individual self-consciousness and transforms it.

Yet there are many things which can prevent us from seeing our common identity. Power in the hands of particular groups and classes serves like a prism to refract reality through their own perspective. Within capitalism the prism of the media creates its own version of revolutionary movements which become incorporated into the revolutionaries' own image of themselves. The outside world invades and distorts revolutionary organizations and consciousness. The hall of mirrors turns itself into a fun palace in which revolutionaries walk continually into bent appearances of themselves. The partial image of a particular oppressed group sometimes even serves to magnify the world of the oppressor by projecting itself at the expense of others who share invisibility. For example, male-dominated black and working-class movements can falsely define their 'manhood' at the expense of women, just as some women define femaleness at the expense of men. They thus cheat themselves and lose the possibility of man-womanhood. They are in the same position as the old woman in the fairy story who was given three wishes and the chance of happiness for ever but was only able to conceive of longings which cancelled out her real desires.

Silence[1]

The oppressed without hope are mysteriously quiet. When the conception of change is beyond the limits of the possible, there are no words to articulate discontent so it is sometimes held not to exist. This mistaken belief arises because we can only grasp silence in the moment in which it is breaking. The sound of

1. This section is based on Sheila Rowbotham, *Women's Liberation and the New Politics*, Spokesman Pamphlet no. 17, originally published by May Day Manifesto Group, summer 1969, now included in *The Body Politic*, Michelene Wandor, Stage 1, 1972.

silence breaking makes us understand what we could not hear before. But the fact that we could not hear does not prove that no pain existed. The revolutionary must listen very carefully to the language of silence. This is particularly important for women because we come from such a long silence.

We perceived ourselves through anecdote, through immediate experience. The world simply was and we were in it. We could only touch and act upon its outer shapes while seeing through the lens men made for us. We had no means of relating our inner selves to an outer movement of things. All theory, all connecting language and ideas which could make us see ourselves in relation to a continuum or as part of a whole were external to us. We had no part in their making. We lumbered around ungainly-like in borrowed concepts which did not fit the shape we felt ourselves to be. Clumsily we stumbled over our own toes, lost in boots which were completely the wrong size. We struggled to do our/their flies up for us/them. We clowned, mimicked, aped our own absurdity. Nobody else took us seriously, we did not even believe in ourselves. We were dolly, chick, broad. We were 'the ladies', 'the girls'. Step forward now dears, let's see you perform. Every time we mounted the steps of their platforms we wanted to run away and hide at home. We had a sense of not belonging. It was evident we were intruders. Those of us who ventured into their territory were most subtly taught our place.

We were allowed to play with their words, their ideas, their culture as long as we pretended we were men. As soon as our cunts bobbed into the light of day, they stiffened, their lips tautened, they seemed to draw themelves into themselves, they cut us down. It was better not to try. One part of ourselves mocked another. We joined in their ridicule of our own aspirations. Either you played their game or you didn't play at all. Part of us leapt over into their world, part of us stayed behind at home. There was a continual temptation to duck out of danger. We were more comfortable doing the washing-up. We retreated, would not be drawn out. We sat silent and accusing when they discussed their theory because it took our men away from us, made them start to impress one another, exposed them to ridicule. We judged them but could never enter the ring ourselves. We made sure we were out of the firing line. We could not bear the responsibility of engagement.

We became bitter and defensive. We disliked ourselves. We were distrustful of other women, particularly those who played their game – the women who did not seem to feel like us. But the distinction was only one of circumstance. Sometimes we were them, sometimes we were playing, performing, acting out our part. Then sometimes we were sunk into ourselves. But always we were split in two, straddling silence, not sure where we would begin to find ourselves or one another. From this division, our material dislocation, came the experience of one part of ourselves as strange, foreign and cut off from the other which we encountered as tongue-tied paralysis about our own identity. We were never all together in one place, we were always in transit, immigrants into alien territory. We felt uncomfortable, watched, ill at ease. The manner in which we knew ourselves was at variance with ourselves as an historical being-woman. Our immediate perceptions of ourselves were locked against our own social potential.

The Nature of Silence

But where was an alternative consciousness of ourselves to come from? We were defined in our paralysis from the first gesture. Simone de Beauvoir makes a beginning. She tries to grasp the process through which the girl-child discovers what it is to be a woman. She explores the learned passivity, the squatting urinating, the discouraged aggression and self-assertion, the energy turned in on itself. The little girl is taught to hold herself in and become 'feminine'. She forces herself into an alien mould. An understanding of how women's consciousness is formed means searching in our most distant memories of ourselves. We still remain very ignorant about the manner in which small children come to self-consciousness. We need to know much more of the specific manner in which particular little girls perceive themselves in particular families in particular forms of society. Equally the process through which the family serves to communicate and reinforce the prevailing values of capitalist society is still only sketchily understood. The generalizations we make about the 'authoritarian' family are manifestly inadequate. The tools we use to perceive consciousness in terms of mass movements are too crude to observe the delicate manner in which human beings stifle and define one another at the point of reproduction. For women at least the location of this consciousness is a matter of some political urgency. It is part of our becoming.

There is also the question of language. As soon as we learn words we find ourselves outside them. To some extent this is a shared exclusion. The word carries a sense of going beyond one's self, theory carries the possibility of connecting and transforming in the realm beyond self. Language conveys a certain power. It is one of the instruments of domination. It is carefully guarded by the superior people because it is one of the means through which they conserve their supremacy.

> In the old days they simply cut off a delinquent's tongue; our society which is more humane lets him keep his organs of phonation on condition that he does not use them ... The truth is that what they fear most is that he may defile words: in like manner, the women of certain tribes must express themselves by gestures; only the men have a right to use speech. If he violates the prohibition, one must neither listen to him nor, above all, answer him ... Obviously they cannot prevent him from speaking soundlessly, in his throat, they cannot prevent him from writing on the walls of his cell, from exchanging signs behind the guards' backs, with the other prisoners: but these furtive, solemn communications confirm him in the feeling that he is stealing language.[2]

The underground language of people who have no power to define and determine themselves in the world develops its own density and precision. It enables them to sniff the wind, sense the atmosphere, defend themselves in a hostile terrain. But it restricts them by affirming their own dependence upon the words of the powerful. It reflects their inability to break out of the imposed reality through to a reality they can define and control for themselves. It keeps them locked against themselves. On the other hand the language of theory – removed language – only expresses

2. J.-P. Sartre, *Saint Genet*, W. H. Allen, 1963, pp. 277–8.

a reality experienced by the oppressors. It speaks only for their world, from their point of view. Ultimately a revolutionary movement has to break the hold of the dominant group over theory, it has to structure its own connections. Language is part of the political and ideological power of the rulers.

There is a long inchoate period during which the struggle between the language of experience and the language of theory becomes a kind of agony. In the making of the working class in Britain the conflict of silence with 'their' language, the problem of paralysis and connection has been continuous. Every man who has worked up through the labour movement expressed this in some form. The embarrassment about dialect, the divorce between home talking and educated language, the otherness of 'culture' – their culture is intense and painful. The struggle is happening now every time a worker on strike has to justify his position in the alien structures of the television studio before the interrogatory camera of the dominant class, or every time a working-class child encounters a middle-class teacher. The degree of accommodation has varied. It has meant sometimes a stilted borrowing from the culture of the ruling class even at the point of denouncing their political and economic hold most fiercely, or it has resulted in a dismissal of theory as something contaminated by belonging to the rulers. The persistent elevation of understanding through direct experience has become both the strength and the weakness of British male-dominated working-class politics. It provides security in the defence of existing strongholds, and weakness in the creation of an offensive strategy. The black movement in America has encountered a similar dilemma.

Although we share the same paralysis, the same estrangement from the world we do not control, the peculiar difficulties we encounter in making words which can become the instruments of our own theory differ. Our oppression is more internalized – the clumsiness of women penetrates the very psyche of our being. It is not just a question of being outside existing language. We can never hope to enter and change it from inside. We can't just occupy existing words. We have to change the meanings of words even before we take them over. Now 'she' represents a woman but 'he' is mankind. If 'she' enters mankind 'she' loses herself in 'he'.

She-he cannot then suddenly become the 'she' she abandoned or the 'she' she wants to become. The present inability of 'she' to speak for more than herself is a representation of reality. 'A man is in the right in being a man, it is the woman who is in the wrong.'[3] It is no good pretending this state of affairs does not exist because we would rather it were not so. The exclusion of women from all existing language demonstrates our profound alienation from any culture which can generalize itself. This is as true of revolutionary consciousness and activity as any other. You can't say to a woman with any conviction and expect her to take herself seriously as a woman, 'Stand up and be a man.' But you can say it to a working-class man or a black man.

Consequently our version of the world has always been fragile and opaque. A woman is repeatedly forced back upon herself. The origin of our oppression, like the roots of all domination, are lost long ago. We are completely without any memory of any alternative. Even the myths of tribes and races of strong women, the golden age of matriarchy, are the creations of male culture. The only means we have of even fantasizing free women is through the projection of male fears. Such women reach our consciousnesses masculinized by the male imagination. We have little part even in the immediate recorded past. We are the background to history. Our present situation imposes fragmentation and isolation. Divided inside and against ourselves and one another we lack both physical and class solidarity. 'They live dispersed among the males attached through residence, housework, economic conditions and social standing to certain men.'[4] The family maintains us in the interior world and the class of our man gives us status in the exterior. We reflect the position they attain. We are social attachments in capitalism.

Moreover, the relationship of man to woman is like no other relationship of oppressor to oppressed. It is far more delicate, far more complex. After all, very often the two love one another. It is a rather gentle tyranny. We are subdued at the very moment of intimacy. Such ecstatic subjugation is thus very different from

3. S. de Beauvoir, *The Nature of the Second Sex*, Four Square, 1968, p. 7.

4. ibid., p. 11.

the relationship between worker and capitalist. The workers can conceive of their own world in the future in which the capitalist no longer figures. We cannot imagine our world in which no men exist. 'The division between the sexes is a biological fact not an event in human history . . . she is the other in a totality of which the two components are necessary to one another.'[5]

Consequently the political emergence of women has to be at once distinct from and in connection to men. But our consciousness of distinctness cannot come just from the external world of work, or the external encounters of life. Female revolutionary consciousness comes from the darkness of our unremembered childhood. Only here does the extent of our colonization become really evident. Think for example how we learn even our psychology and physiology from our oppressors. We substitute our own experience of our genitals, our menstruation, our orgasm, our menopause, for an experience determined by men. We are continually translating our own immediate fragmented sense of what we feel into a framework which is constructed by men. The particular sensations of women have the quality of the exceptional. It is as if everything that relates only to us comes out in footnotes to the main text, as worthy of the odd reference. We come on the agenda somewhere between 'Youth' and 'Any other business'. We encounter ourselves in men's culture as 'by the way' and peripheral. According to all the reflections we are not really there. This puzzles us and means it is harder for us to begin to experience our own identity as a group. This gives female consciousness an elusive and disintegrating feeling. We are the negative to their positive. We are oppressed by an overwhelming sense of not being there.

Every time a woman describes to a man any experience which is specific to her as a woman she confronts his recognition of his own experience as normal. More than this, his experience of how he sees the 'norm' is reinforced by the dominant ideology which tells both him and the woman that he is right. This inability to find ourselves in existing culture as we experience ourselves is true of course for other groups besides women. The working class, blacks, national minorities within capitalism all encounter them-

5. ibid.

selves as echoes, they lose themselves in the glitter and gloss of the images capitalism projects to them.

However, the problem for women is particularly internalized. This is partly a matter of history. We have no time or place to look back to. The movement we have created to liberate *all* women is incomparably weaker than the labour movement: historically we have sought 'brotherhood'; we are still 'Yours fraternally'. We have not unravelled what we share and what is specific to us.

Equally this internalization is a matter of anatomy and physiology. The sexual distinction at once binds us closely to our oppressors and distinguishes us more sharply from them. This does not mean that we are not more than our biology but it does mean that our difference is penetrated immediately at a level of sensation and experience which does not relate just to the external world. It means also that the exploration of the internal areas of consciousness is a political necessity for us. However, men – especially revolutionary men – often fail to see this. They have defined politics for themselves as something which belongs to the external realm. It is to do with strikes, mass meetings, demonstrations. Their revolution has a symbolism for the outer shape of things and the inner world goes along on the old tracks. But this is an incomplete picture; we know, not as an abstract idea, but from our experience of our specific material situation, that our consciousness as women is inseparable from our relation to the encounters of our anatomy. This is true of childbirth and of sexuality – after all, a man enters us through our vagina; we perceive his body through our sensation of him on top or underneath, inside and outside. The manner in which we touch each other in bed is part of the way in which we learn about ourselves.

Men often speak with amusement about our preoccupation with the orgasm. They brandish it as a sign of our inability to understand the serious world of their politics, but in so doing they suffer from a failure of imagination common among dominant groups. This is part of the way in which they have been hobbled themselves. Both we and they have to recognize the limitations of their perspective. The exploration of our own sexuality is a crucial factor in the creation of a revolutionary female consciousness. We have to rediscover our whole selves, not simply the selves which slot into the existing male world, and the way to start is by communicating with one another. Without a political movement it is barely possible for women to describe even how they experience their own sexuality. It is only a conscious relationship to other women which will encourage us to trust our own isolated, atomized and fragmented sensations.

Our cultural colonization extends not just to sex, but even to illness, and the whole half-articulated world of gynaecological complaints. For example, if a woman goes to a doctor complaining of period pains, cystitis, or depression during her menopause, her experience of them will lose itself in male non-experience of them. This male non-experience in the shape of the individual doctor and his science which is the embodiment of the non-experiences of the past will bear down upon her experience to persuade her that she can't possibly really feel as ill as she says. Behind the male non-experience of female experience lurks the rationalization that women always exaggerate their complaints. When someone steadfastly refuses to hear you, you respond by turning up the amplification. When workers do this they are dismissed blandly as unreasonable and ignorant. When women do this we are regarded as unreasonable, ignorant *and* hysterical. We step neatly into another male dismissive 'non-experience' – hysteria or the view from the womb. The political implications of this have been exposed by women's liberation in relation to childbirth, contraception and abortion. Our lack of control over our own bodies matches the workers's lack of control over production.

Breaking the Silence

When a man curls his lip, when he uses ridicule, when he grows angry, you have touched a raw nerve in domination. Men will often admit other women are oppressed but not you. Well it was true in the past but not now, well yes they are in Liverpool but not in London or wherever you live. Gradually you will force them nearer home. Then they will stick. They will accuse you of rocking the boat, they will demand loyalty to their particular group or party. They will tell you to be patient. They will say you criticize the behaviour of men in a personal rather than in a political way. If you are working-class they'll humiliate you with your sex and class ignorances, if you are middle-class they'll call you a petty bourgeois deviationist. We must not be discouraged by them. We must go our own way but remember we are going to have to take them with us. They learn slowly. They are like creatures who have just crawled out of their shells after millennia of protection. They are sore and tender and afraid.

It is impossible to confront a common condition before you have discovered it. The first stage in this discovery is the recognition by the oppressed of a general situation of domination. You can't begin to find your own power until you have consciously recognized your non-power. It is evident that the idea of female oppression is not new. Nor is the concept of male hegemony. Karen Horney quotes the philosopher Georg Simmel, for example, in her paper of 1926, 'The Flight from Womanhood', as saying that all existing culture is male-defined and that the very notion of objectivity can be equated with masculinity. Simmel stated that the standards of estimating male and female nature were not 'neutral ... but essentially masculine'. He showed how this was concealed by the naïve identification of the concept 'human being' and the concept 'man' in some languages and noted that 'in the most varying fields, inadequate achievements are contemptuously called "feminine", while distinguished achievements on the part of women are called "masculine" as an expression of praise'.[6]

Karen Horney related this realization to her study of psychology. She recognized the elements of domination in all existing male-defined ideology. 'At any given time, the more powerful side will create an ideology suitable to help maintain its position and to make this position acceptable to the weaker one. In this ideology the differentness of the weaker one will be interpreted as inferiority, and it will be proven that these differences are unchangeable, basic, or God's will. It is the function of such an

6. Georg Simmel, *Philosophische Kultur*, in Karen Horney, *Feminine Psychology*, ed. Harold Kelman, Routledge & Kegan Paul, 1967, p. 56.

ideology to deny or conceal the existence of a struggle.'[7] She added that the unawareness of the existence of conflict between the sexes was a result of its concealment by male-dominated culture and the acceptance by women of such a culture. This concealment should be understood not in terms of a conscious plot but as a way of seeing the world which comes directly from a specific material situation which the rulers seek to maintain. The particularity of this world view is obscured. The dominant group sees itself as indistinguishable from civilization.

Simone de Beauvoir takes up the same theme. 'The truth is that man today represents the positive and the neutral – that is to say, the male and the human being – whereas woman is only the negative, the female, whenever she behaves as a human being she is declared to be identifying herself with the male.'[8] She shows how it is a completely unnatural procedure for the 'female human being to make herself a feminine woman' and adds that her sense of inferiority is not a product of her imagination but of her actual social predicament. 'Woman feels inferior because, in fact, the requirements of femininity *do* belittle her. She spontaneously chooses to be a complete person, a subject and a free being with the world and the future open before her. If this choice is confused with virility, it is so to the extent that femininity today means mutilation.'[9]

Once grasped at a general level ideas become like a kind of shorthand in our consciousness. But it is one thing to encounter a concept, quite another to understand it. In order to understand a general idea like male hegemony it is necessary first to perceive in a whole series of separate moments how this has affected you. Then those moments have to be communicated. This is part of the total process of female self-recognition. It is the way through which we start to make our own language, and discover our own reflections. The confirmation of our understanding comes through our organization and our action.

My own realization of the depth and extent of my colonization came with the force of an electric shock. It jolted me into per-

7. Horney, op. cit., p. 116.
8. S. de Beauvoir, *The Second Sex*, p. 147.
9. ibid.

ceiving all my glimpses of myself in a different light. I had always dreaded all those aspects of myself which might resemble Mathieu's mistress in Sartre's *The Age of Reason*. I looked with contempt at other women who appeared to be sunk into their bodies as she was. I carried this dread around with me and watched my flesh as I grew older for signs that I was becoming like her. One day it occurred to me that she didn't exist as a woman at all. She was merely the creation of a man's projected fears about the things a woman could do to him. He was just a man like any other: a man who was afraid of being stifled by a woman's body. When I realized this I experienced a kind of joy like that which Bunyan describes when Christian's burden rolls off. I felt incomparably light-spirited. My eyes opened a bit wider. It became easier to see that this was a general state of affairs. We learn ourselves through women made by men. A man is not a male film-maker, or a male writer. He is simply a film-maker or a writer. It is all a clever sleight of hand. Even our fears of what we might become are from them.

But I was still rather complacent about my independence. I felt I did not try to please men. Of course I did really but not in ways which could immediately be seen. I'd never washed shirts and darned socks. I had always shared housework with men. When I went to the film *Bonnie and Clyde* I noticed rather smugly how she did her hair in the way he told her. Her face so pathetically took her cue from him. 'I'd never submit so meekly,' I thought. 'I'd have much more pride than that.' The thought was scarcely out of my head when the man who was with me turned to me innocently and said, 'She looks just like you often look.' I'd always thought I knew when I was acting 'feminine'. Apparently it was quite out of my control.

I had yet to understand the extent to which I identified with men, used their eyes. I was really sliced in two. Half of me was like a man surveying the passive half of me as a woman-thing. On Boxing Day in 1967 the Beatles' *Magical Mystery Tour* appeared on television. A group of people including the Beatles go on a coach trip. There is the atmosphere of excitement of all being on the bus together and of enjoying a treat. When they get off all kinds of things happen: tugs-of-war which remind you of the desperate tugging you felt you had to do when you were a child; a woman who eats and eats and cries and cries until you can't imagine how a human being could carry so many tears around inside her. Then at one point all the boys in the bus are separated from the girls. You follow the boys in the film, wriggling around in your seat in front of the telly, in mounting excitement. It's like going into the Noah's Ark at Blackpool when you're six or listening to very loud rock music when you're thirteen. I got the same tightening down at the bottom of my spine. Well there I was clenching my cunt and where should they go but into a striptease. I had caught myself going to watch another woman as if I were a man. I was experiencing the situation of another woman stripping through men's eyes. I was being asked to desire myself by a film made by men. Catching myself observing myself desiring one of my selves I remained poised for an instant in two halves. But as soon as she started to sing a song which said she'd make you pay for everything you got, I started to laugh. She was not at all frightening to me. But she was frightening to them – she was outside them. They wanted her. I only half-wanted to be like her. She symbolized an attractive woman but it was the kind of woman I'd very early on decided I wouldn't be like. Because her only weapon was her charade at the fair she had to make them pay for it. This was her way of surviving. I had other ways. I had no need to sell myself directly as a commodity. However, she was also not frightening because I knew the gestures she made to excite them from inside. I knew how to drop into the stereotypes we learn as female sexuality. I was familiar with the woman they feared. I could see through their eyes but I could feel with her body. I was a man-woman. I had thus contributed towards making an object of myself and other women. I was partly responsible for our degradation.

In the absence of a political movement we become accomplices. This is a further complexity in the microcosm of domination. Simone de Beauvoir notes some of the inducements to complicity, the manner in which the delights of passivity are made to seem desirable to the young girl. In isolation the individual woman who passes over into activity is bound to define herself at the expense of other women. This is apparent at the level of class. The freedom of the emancipated upper-class woman is simply the other side of the unfreedom of the working-class woman who supports her. But it exists also in terms of sex. The emancipated educated woman is untouchable; she acquires an asexual protected dignity which is the reverse of the closeness of the traditional woman to her body. Individually either she accepts this situation or she attempts to enter the body of the woman who is still passive. As part of you leaps outside yourself, another part tries to re-enter a self you have created in your own imagination. You make for yourself a stereotype of suffering womanhood and let it bleed. You dwell continually on your female troubles. When you sleep with a man you enjoy him forcing you to submit. You are torn between shame and delight. 'She simultaneously longs for and dreads the shameful passivity of the willing prey.'[10] We exult in the very moment of mutilation. We are encouraged in our masochism by male stereotypes. A whole flock of patient, bruised, black-eyed Griseldas passes through the pages of history. We mistakenly believe that when we have taken all suffering to ourselves we will no longer feel pain, that we are indestructible because we survive a degradation of our own choice and making. 'Woman assumes her most delicious triumphs by first falling into the depths of abjection; whether God or a man is concerned; the little girl learns that she will become all-powerful through deepest resignation; she takes delight in a masochism that promises supreme conquests.'[11]

To recognize that we are the victims of our own masochism is our political beginning. We can't begin to find our way without the help of other women and ultimately without help from men. We can only break the hold of masochism when we experience the collective self-assertion of a movement for liberation. But we will only realize our own new collectivity by connecting politically with other groups who are oppressed.

10. ibid., p. 62.
11. ibid., p. 33.

Men

Men sense the contradiction in us. They observe our desire to be prey. They notice how we want to put ourselves in their hands, to be overwhelmed, pinned down by them. They encourage feminine allurements by demanding to be lured and thus obliging women to offer to men the myth of submission. But equally by desiring them when they make us submit we make it impossible for them to glimpse their manhood as anything which is not cruel and conquering. They are ashamed of their own sensitivity to suffering and love because they have been taught to regard these as feminine. They are afraid of becoming feminine because this means that other men will despise them, we will despise them and they will despise themselves. Men are as afraid of being rejected and despised as we are. They have only a defensive solidarity. In face of the positive solidarity we make through a movement they have only the reaction of the traditional male world. Those who are revolutionaries can recognize this to be oppressive to women but they have no practical way out yet. The remains of passivity in women still means that sometimes men find themselves lured out into the open and admitting their sense of dislocation only to find themselves humiliated and misused. They close up on us. They became impatient with our unevenness. In our fantasy life we submit even as in our real life we resist. In their fantasy life they resist even as in their real life they submit. We must keep the dialectic open. If we tighten on them they will be afraid for their identity, but if we let them go they will try and shake off responsibility. We are moving towards a new world together but development is an uneven and painful process. We must be honest and help one another until they find a new way to express and organize themselves towards us. The generalization of our consciousness of our own subordination enables them to discover a new manner of being men.

The Politics of the Irrational

There are innumerable areas of experience to which our understanding of political class consciousness does not extend. For instance it is not clear what is the relationship between dreams, fantasy, visions, orgasm, love and the revolution. There is a tendency to dismiss these vital aspects of our lives because they are not easily understood in existing political terms. But as long as we continue to dismiss them we cannot work out what effect they have on our actions. This makes it difficult to predict the consequences of things. It is necessary to understand the relationship between our experience in fantasy, dream and ecstasy and the experience which is intelligible to us in terms of political strategy. This is most evident to women because it is clear to us that our consciousness of our orgasms is part not only of the total relationship with the men we are with, but also of our total situation in relation to our bodies, other women, and the world outside. All these materially affect the nature and scope of orgasm. Not only does the general communicate to the particular, the particular defines the course of the general way things are. An essential part of our political emergence is to discover our own particularity, but we are continually taught to distrust the particular feeling that does not fit. If we are to go on and change things we have to do more than grasp this theoretically. 'Knowing the cause of a passion is not enough to overcome it, one must live it, one must oppose other passions to it, one must combat it tenaciously, in short one must work oneself over.' [12]

I glimpsed this first through my relationship to mascara. It was so important to me I would not be seen without it. I felt ashamed at my own triviality in men's eyes. I could not explain the nature of my fears in a way which was sensible to them. I recognized this was insoluble in terms of 'reason':

> It is not a question of simply rational enlightenment. Intellectual awareness of what is going on does not mean object-consciousness dissolves. When I go without mascara on my eyes I experience myself as I knew myself before puberty. It is inconceivable to me that any

12. J.-P. Sartre, *The Problem of Method*, Methuen, 1964, p. 12.

man could desire me sexually, my body hangs together quite differently. Rationally I can see the absurdity of myself. But this does not mean I experience myself in a different way.[13]

It was not the mascara that was important. This would be to make a fetish of it. It was my relationship to it. But I was not able to modify my relationship to it until other versions of other women's relationships to their artificially created femininity had served to reinforce and extend my own perception of this particular part of myself. A few years ago I was barely able to describe it on paper. I had to fight all my sense of what was a 'serious' political matter. I had been unable to connect the politics I learned from men to the politics of my mother's bedroom, the secret world where I watched her again and again 'putting on her face'. The existence of a women's political movement makes possible such new distinctions and new connections.

In order for Marxism to prove useful as a revolutionary weapon for women, we have at once to encounter it in its existing form and fashion it to fit our particular oppression. This means extending it into areas in which men have been unable to take it by distilling it through the particularities of our own experience. Our own situation is rich in the most bizarre of complexities and combinations and we must translate these strange phenomena of female life as we now live it into the language of theory. This theoretical consciousness will inevitably be confused when so much of ourselves remains opaque. But discouragement should not goad us into the trap of presenting our reality according to an already existing scheme of abstraction. By such false conceits we would only mislead one another. Such short cuts will only waste time. We are fortunate to live in a time when new connections and communications are becoming possible, when all manner of people who had previously been 'trodden in the dirt, people with no place in society, people with no right to speak have audaciously lifted up their heads [and] taken power into their hands'.[14]

13. Sheila Rowbotham, *Women's Liberation and The New Politics*, Spokesman Pamphlet no. 17, p. 27.

14. Mao Tse-tung, 'Investigation of Peasant Movement in Hunan', *Selected Readings*, Collet's, 1968.

Amidst this great movement of the riff-raff we have much to learn. But we must remember to transmit too our story of our own most precious distinctions as we move from passivity and silence through the looking-glass of history into communism.

PART 2

What Did You Do Today, Dear?

According to the materialist conception the determining factor in history is, in the final instance, the production and reproduction of the immediate essentials of life. This again is of a two-fold character. On the one side, the production of the means of existence, articles of food and clothing, dwellings and of the tools necessary for that production; on the other side, the production of human beings themselves, the propagation of the species. The social organization under which the people of a particular historical epoch and a particular country live is determined by both kinds of production: by the stage of development of labour on the one hand and of the family on the other.

F. Engels,
Preface to *The Origin of The Family*, 1884

What did you do today, dear, what did you do today?

I've been nailing gentle tacks into my soft coffin
sucking sweet dust in an endless lust
hoovering manoeuvring
weird shrieks out of every room
I pressed out life's creases in your crumpled clothes
spent two tangible hours with Jimmy Young
washed sorrow down my gullet with a long, oversweetened draught of
song
waited for a vision . . .
when the telly goes wrong, I don't know what to do
the children accuse me with their violent eyes for not being you
everywhere i turn
i find
dull unfinished beginnings
of my mind

I've hung listless on an upturned spike
waiting for wind
the world turns in its own breeze.
I know nothing of your hurricanes and worldly tornadoes
my winds are zephyrs
and zephyrs are not winds at all
but promises
of embraces...

Yes, but what did you DO today, dear, what did you DO today?

Pat van Twest in *Enough*, June 1970,
Bristol Women's Liberation Group.

is delineated by a power structure in which the man with nothing to sell but his labour is subordinate to the people who own capital and have the law on their side. Their law gives them the 'right' to take away by force if necessary part of what he produces. Technology either in the form of machines or rationalization of the work process is designed not to improve the nature of work but to smooth the path for the extraction of profit in whatever form from the worker. His exploitation is tangible. He can see and feel the appropriation and the expenditure of himself.

The world of work occupies the worker body and soul for eight hours a day. Leisure is time not at work. It is what is left over to him. Leisure is time in which he is allowed to recover himself. But in fact the separation of work and leisure is a fragile one. A man can't switch off eight hours of his activity when he clocks out. The capitalist production process does not only occupy its operators at work, it pursues them in their rest, in their family, in bed, in their dreams. Do dreams change on Saturday night? Do strikes change the pattern of dreaming? Work is something to live your life around. Love is something to be squeezed in between.

Capitalism has its own 'realism'. It brags in the universities of its 'social science'. It is continually up to new tricks. Shift work, piece work, bonus schemes, productivity deals. It erodes continually the carefully cleared areas of bargaining power, patiently and laboriously gained by pressure from the shop floor and the stewards. One of its recent devices is the three-shift system. This is designed to keep expensive machinery running continually. It means the rhythm of work changes all the time instead of remaining constant. The repeated alteration of the work shift wears into men. The tension, internalized to an even greater extent than normal night work, comes home into the family. Workers on the weekly rotating shift can't sleep properly, it affects their appetite, they feel tired, get constipated. Instead of simply the adjustment to a constant pattern of work, the rhythm alters, but the control of work time is still not in the hands of the worker. The results are physical and social. Ulcers, rheumatoid arthritis, respiratory infections, headaches and rectal complaints are capitalism's accumulated debt of exhausted human tissue. The toll extracted recognizes no limitation. Amidst all the sanctimony of respect for personal life and the need to conserve the family, the capitalist organization of work, whose criterion is the profitable production of commodities for the market, proceeds to penetrate the private world of the family, making a mockery of its own protestations.

A study of German workers, for instance, shows the extent to which shift work disrupts family life.

> The most frequently mentioned difficulties in husband-wife relationships concern the absence of the worker from the home in the evening, sexual relations, and difficulties encountered by the wife in carrying out her household duties. Another area of family life that seems to be adversely affected by certain kinds of shift work is the father-child relationship.[1]

The capitalist mode of production determines family life also by its failure to make enough houses for people to live in, or towns which are designed round the needs of people living in them, by high rents and harmful food, by schools which act as its domestic magistrate, by medical services which are both inadequate and autocratic. It builds tower blocks like Ronan Point which collapse; it builds flats with thin walls where children cannot play. It cramps workers into small spaces. At the slightest threat to the mess it has thrown up it responds with a sickly self-righteousness playing off women against men, men against women. It utilizes the separation it has created between consumption and production to pretend that it is an inevitable law that wage increases are passed on in price increases, and that profits are always by-passed. So the working class pays for every rise in its standard of living. This is the truth in the saying 'The rich get richer and the poor get poorer'. No strike is complete without the tear-jerking article about the suffering resentful wives who have 'to pinch and scrape and queue and trudge and fetch and carry and worry'.[2] Strikers are upbraided for 'penaliz-

1. P. E. Mott, *Shift Work: The Social, Psychological and Physical Consequences*, University of Michigan, Ann Arbor, 1965, p. 18; quoted in Tony Cliff, *The Employers' Offensive*, Pluto Press, 1970, p. 71.

2. Anne Edwards, *Sunday Express*, 19 July 1970.

ing the women and children'. Nobody seemed to have any feelings for the women and children before the men went on strike. The ruling class grows sentimental at its own convenience.

In the case of the middle-class man the family is determined by the external world of work in a rather different way. While his work will usually be physically easier than the factory worker's, he is subjected to complex psychological pressures. He is fearful always about his own ability to compete successfully; he feels obliged to make better and better provision for his family. Probably under pressure from his wife to push himself ahead, he will have few friends because in the search for better prospects he has moved around, or the seniority of his position makes intimacy embarrassing. At work he won't know who to trust and he'll always be conscious of being somehow watched, at home he will feel undermined by his wife's desperate ambition that can only express itself through his material achievement.

The family as a place of retreat and sexuality as a means of release become increasingly important as compensatory ideals as capitalism makes both retreat and release impossible within the world of work. Although in need of protection from different circumstances, both working-class and middle-class men combine to secure their sanctuary. The condition of the preservation of the 'ideal' family as of the 'ideal' fuck are definitions of female nature which are not only imposed, but imposed in order to maintain the interest men have in finding compensation from the exploitation and alienation capitalism forces on them at work. Continuance of this situation produces not only a distorted reality in the family and a continual source of aggression and resentment as human beings fail to live up to their impossible ideal stereotypes of one another, it allows the values of commodity production to mould and determine aspects of human experience which are apparently completely separate from work.

The family and sexuality serve not only as safety and release mechanisms but also pick up and transmit versions of capitalist society, they reinforce the world of work and consumption. Men and women devour their children, regarding them as property; they use their 'love' as blackmail, care becomes an investment. 'After all I've done for you.' Parents hit their children for their own good because their parents did it to them. In old age they have recourse to masochism and their children treat them as a liability. Human beings put up a deceitful parade of self-importance and all-knowingness because they have been taught that no one will respect them if they don't. They grow a skin which is as hard and thick as that of a rhinoceros in order to distinguish themselves to themselves. They set themselves apart by their own posturing about the need for authority. By authority they mean merely the power to crush another human being as they once were crushed. Even a worm will turn they say, but whoever decided worms were to be lowly in the first place? Shulamith Firestone describes how children too have suffered from having 'purity' imposed upon them as have women. 'Their inferior status was ill-concealed under an elaborate "respect".'[3] Within the middle-class family particularly the 'helplessness' and 'incapacity' foisted onto the woman and children allow the man to exercise benevolent paternalism.

Even this form of patronage is coming on to the cash-nexus. Describing a piece of market research for an American life insurance firm Ernest Dichter eloquently expresses the tendency within capitalism for all relationships to be reduced to a cash estimate:

> The very act of giving, in buying life insurance, cuts through the childhood pattern of love. By the same token he also thinks in terms of larger units: his wife, his family. He identifies himself with them even beyond death ... The amount of money a man has decided to invest in the happiness of his wife and family reflects, on a deeper level, the amount of sexual power he is capable of mustering and investing in making her happy. This is easily understood when one realizes that money and power are to a large extent identified in our culture, and that a man's 'power' is in itself an ambiguous term implying position as well as potency.[4]

The variations of this are infinite. Presumably men working in a factory where time-and-motion studies are used to raise productivity must be induced to conceive their sexual capacity in terms

3. Shulamith Firestone, *The Dialectic of Sex*, Jonathan Cape, 1971, p. 99.
4. Ernest Dichter, *The Strategy of Desire*, Boardman, 1960, p. 221.

of the speed of the operation – the proverbial 'once in and wipe it'.

This is not to say that all human emotion is impossible but that our most personal, private experiences are affected by the external social relations. It is true that sexual pleasure is particularly resistant to the bourgeois yardstick of achievement, the work discipline of supervision and stop-watch. Indeed, in the attempt to translate the capitalist ethic into the orgasm, the orgasm has tended to show a remarkable ability to go its own way. In the most bizarre circumstances human beings show a potentiality for delight, a strength to arch into light, to leap out of their own skins and simultaneously be more themselves than they have ever been allowed to dare, to cleave to one another without the need to smother and clutch. But such moments remain as particular experiences *despite* the prevailing notions of sexuality or love. They are against the way things are. Because ownership and possession are general in society it means that the relations between parents and children, women and men, will carry traces of that tendency of human beings to destroy and devour one another.

The manifestations of the specific manner in which the dominant relations and values of capitalist society penetrate all the supposedly 'personal' areas of human life are still largely unexplored. The political expression of personal experience was traditionally confined to novels and poetry. Lenin told Inessa Armand that discussion of free love was out of place in a pamphlet. Psychoanalysis, the science of personal experience, is only tentatively revolutionary. Anti-psychiatry is still very young. It is really women's liberation and gay liberation which have insisted that the personal is political and have begun to describe and analyse some of the implications. Sometimes the expression of male sexuality in the language of commodity production is particularly blatant. Kate Millett describes Henry Miller's reduction of sexuality into quantifiable experience in terms of acquisition and achievement:

As sex, or rather 'cunt', is not only merchandise but a monetary species, Miller's adventures read like so many victories for sharp practice, carry the excitement of a full ledger, and operate on the flat premise that quantity is quality. As with any merchant whose sole concern is profit, the 'goods' themselves grow dull and contemptible, and even the amassing of capital pales beside the power it becomes.[5]

This idea of sex as accumulation appears frequently in advertising. Accumulation brings freedom.

The competitive values of capitalism mean that men acquire their sexual identity as something to be defended against all comers. Sexual performance becomes a goal which the man has to strive towards. For Norman Mailer sexual encounters are the last staggering bouts of a boxer with old scores and deep scars whose buddies have deserted their seats round the ring. Every hard-on is the straining desperate achievement in destruction of a hero trapped by the impossibility of heroism in the world as it is. Even when male-defined sexuality is a release from acquisition and competition it reproduces the world outside in its own idiom. It translates the values of work and money into passion.

The other side of this is the sacred romantic ideal which pretends the passionate self can be separated from earning a living, and idealizes women in order to avoid encountering them as people. The power to impose the notion of the family, childhood, femininity, sexuality as apart and distinct from the general harsh, competitive world outside in which only men are strong enough to rule, serves to reinforce and maintain capitalism. The economic control of the man in the family within the division of labour now enables statements like 'The Englishman's home is his castle', 'A man must be master in his own home', 'I go out when I like, my wife goes out when I tell her', to continue at once to reflect the existing reality and to secure it. Women take it out on a man in the only way they can, they sneer at militancy at work, because this makes a man less a provider and more his own man. They sense a distorted notion of manhood and hit where he is weakest. They allow men to play at being supermen, even to put on the coat of King Kong, because this façade of masculinity can still be manipulated by traditional tactics. It is when the man tries to stop playing, to be a 'man' without any false power, that

5. Kate Millett, *Sexual Politics*, Hart Davis, 1971, p. 299.

women helpless to assert themselves any other way have sometimes rubbed his nose in his own ignobility. This can sometimes be when he is straining towards a new identity through solidarity, and a new dignity through brotherhood. The woman is both excluded and threatened by such action. The role of women in the family within capitalism is structured so that the removal of male patronage leaves her exposed and terrified. Consequently she tries to force him to stay confined within the tiny, carefully polished, endlessly cleaned territory of the family – her world. She seeks to trap the man and bind him down, just as the way that life is organized in capitalism has trapped and bound her.

In the bourgeois mind for which the ways of capitalism are ahistorical, inevitable and eternal, this conflict appears either as essentially a tragedy in which the liberation of women is an obscure and religious affair, or the sex-war is presented as a timeless comedy in which the characters swop roles, hide under the bed, come out in drag, camp it, buffoon it, burlesque it. Both these serve to perpetuate the existing state of affairs as mystery.

Antagonism between men and women is thus actually built into the separation of the point of production from the point of consumption, which was a product of capitalism's organization of work. The appropriation of the wage-earner's capacity for creative activity by capital is accompanied by the distortion of relations between human beings in the family and in sexuality. Although capitalist ideology presents this as biological and beyond the power of human beings to transform, in fact the particular manner in which women are oppressed within the family in capitalism is an historical aspect of one form of society only. The nature of female subordination is as subject to social change as any other kind of subordination. Women were oppressed before capitalism. But capitalism has changed the nature of female oppression.

The organization of production within capitalism creates a separate and segmented vision of life which continually restricts consciousness of alternatives. People perceive themselves in opposition to one another. The family's isolation serves to maintain this. Women often see themselves in terms of this social isolation. Even their dreams are lonely and circumscribed, 'Everyone's alone really, aren't they? No one can help me except Ernie. All I want is a garden, I've got a nice home. My dream's a cottage in the country, with a garden . . . I suppose some women aren't strong enough and need a push. I don't need to beg so I don't need a group. My husband would give anything he would – after all it's his duty to supply all my needs.'[6]

While men continue to find self-esteem through dominance in the family or in bed, their notion of democracy at work is continually dissipated. A purely economic consciousness at the point of production remains incapable of a theoretical offensive against commodity production.

> The tendency of male workers to think of themselves as men (i.e. powerful) rather than as workers (i.e. members of an oppressed group), promotes a false sense of privilege and power, and an identification with the world of men, including the boss. The petty dictatorship which most men exercise over their wives and families enables them to vent their anger and frustration in a way which poses no challenge to the system. The role of the man in the family reinforces aggressive individualism, authoritarianism and a hierarchical view of social relations, values which are fundamental to the perpetuation of capitalism.[7]

Thus when the ruling class grows sanctimonious about the preservation of the family they mean in fact the need to preserve the division of labour which best secures profit. When they wax eloquent on the 'natural' role of women, they mean the ideal of naturalness which capitalism manufactures for itself as it makes an increasingly unnatural and polluted world in which human beings are bred to produce rather than production organized in the interests of human beings.

The sexual division of labour means that men and women are at different points in the structure of social relationship. Men as a group have a different relation from women as a group to the means of production. Women enter commodity production, and, like men, produce goods which circulate as commodities; they

6. 'Housewives Talking', *Shrew*, Vol. 3, no. 5, June 1971, pp. 1–2.

7. Kathy McAfee and Myrna Wood, 'Bread and Roses', reprinted from *Leviathan* by Agitprop, London, 1969, p. 2.

thus share the exploitation and experience of alienation of male workers in capitalism. But, because within the social division of labour in capitalism the task of maintaining and reproducing commodity producers is largely given to women, the expenditure of female labour power in procreation and in the nourishing of men and children at home determines how much female labour can be expended in the production of commodities. Thus, while the conditions of production outside penetrate and shape the nature of production and reproduction in the family, both materially and psychologically, the family mode of production also affects commodity production. It acts both to maintain and to restrict the exploitation of labour power by capital.

Relations outside are maintained partly by the separation of male/female roles, by the values of authority and competition, and partly by the family as an ideal, a human alternative to the inhumanity of social relations at work. The family is a place of sanctuary for all the hunted, jaded, exhausted sentiments out of place in commodity production. Chased out of the dominant mode of production where there is no room for emotion, such characteristics as love, tenderness and compassion assume a mawkish guise from confinement. The family is thus in one sense the dummy ideal, the repository of ghostly substitutes, emotional fictions which dissolve into cloying sentimentality or explode into thrashing, battering, remorseless violence.

But this distortion of human relations still represents the only possibility of personal life. The family is the only place where human beings find whatever continuing love, security and comfort they know. In an unloving, insecure and comfortless society, not surprisingly people value this aspect of the family even if they rebel against the enclosing and twisting characteristics which are inherent in the intensity of the nuclear family unit. Thus unless changes in the family are part of changes in society as a whole people will resist being cut off from the place they can hide in and the place in which they can be vulnerable. This is the case also with love between couples, though in a less structured form. Thus while it is true that love relationships between men and women, or men and men, or women and women, can reproduce the competition outside, or become dummy ideals, it is also true that while the rest of society remains as it is people value even their distorted personal selves. Personal life is not separate from public life, intimacy is not exempt from the penetration of the values of capitalism, merely by physical seclusion, but we have to be careful that by a purely negative attack on the retreats and release which capitalism allows we do not expose people to the inhumanity of cash values.

The family does not only serve to maintain capitalist commodity production, it also serves to restrict its expansion – hence the ambiguity of 'personal' life. From the point of view of the continuing self-expansion of capital the family acts as an irrational brake. This has appeared in several ways. Since the industrial revolution there has been continuing friction between the working-class family, no longer the place of production for the man, and work in industry. The family could not compete with the factory. The restrictive role of the family was evident in the nineteenth century, both ideologically and socially, where the values of the family were local as opposed to national, antagonistic to centralization and the growth of the authority of the state. The state, guarding the long-term interests of capitalist production, made education compulsory and prevented parents from sending their children out to work. By the second half of the nineteenth century capital was beginning to need a literate work force and could not afford the exhaustion of human tissue which child labour involved. The campaigners against child labour and for state education forced capitalism to rationalize itself.

The twentieth-century nuclear family represented a compromise. It is a much less unwieldy and awkward unit than the complex kinship network characteristic of a society in which people stayed in the same place and station all their lives. But as the family became smaller in size its emotional load became heavier. The monogamous nuclear family has become such a preposterous ideal that it sags with the weight of its unrealized hopes almost before it creates itself.

But although the nuclear family was fashioned for capitalism's needs it retains many archaic qualities. The old-worldliness of the family is not an affair of chance, but continues because the family not only serves to maintain capitalism ideologically but is itself still a place of production, even though the scope and nature of that production have been diminished. Female production in the family means that the commodity producer, the husband, and the future producers, the children, survive to produce commodities which are exchanged. The separation of male/female roles is thus materially as well as ideologically part of the way in which capitalism is maintained. Female production in the family differs from production in industry because it is still for immediate use. It differs also from the production in the family before industrialization. Goods were produced at home for exchange then. This is no longer general. The values which come from this female mode of production have a different quality from the dominant values in capitalism; gentle, unaggressive, caring, decent, fatalistic, afraid of change, conservative and isolated, they always seem to be backward-looking.

> Since bourgeois society is only a form resulting from the development of antagonistic elements, some relations belonging to earlier forms of society are frequently to be found in a crippled state or as a travesty of their former self, as for example communal property.[8]

Men and women are brought up for a different position in the labour force: the man for the world of work, the woman for the family. This difference in the sexual division of labour in society means that the relationship of men as a group to production is different from that of women. For a man the social relations and values of commodity production predominate and home is a retreat into intimacy. For the woman the public world of work belongs to and is owned by men. She is dependent on what the man earns but is responsible for the private sphere, the family. In the family she does a different kind of work from the man. The family now only rarely produces goods for exchange. Instead the woman's production is for immediate use. The social relationships in the family mode of production are different from those outside, although they hinge upon commodity production. Thus these differences in the way in which production is structured serve to shape the consciousness of men and women. In the case of

8. D. McLellan, *Marx's Grundrisse*, MacMillan, 1970, pp. 39–40.

women who go out to work, the main responsibility is still the home.

In the relation of husband and wife there is an exchange of services which resembles the bond between man and man in feudalism. The woman essentially serves the man in exchange for care and protection, though the specific balance between them is personally determined. Within feudalism the serf served his lord in return for the obligation of protection from physical assault, however the particular nature of dependency varied. Sometimes the bond between man and man was relatively loose, and limited by emerging rights. In the case of the lower orders it carried traces of servility because the obligation passed to the dependents.

> About early vassalage, based on the group of armed followers gathered about the chief, there was a sort of cosy domestic flavour, which was expressed in its very vocabulary. The master was 'the old man' (*senior*, *heir*) or the giver of orders (*lord*); the men were his companions (*gassindi*), his boys (*vassi*, *thegns*, knights), his bread eaters (*buccellani*, *hlafoetam*). Fealty, in short, was based at that time on personal contact and subjection shaded off into comradeship . . .
>
> As it extended beyond the household the bond became at once looser but more clearly determined in opposition to rights. It was impossible any longer to impose 'quasi domestic loyalty'. Eventually this fealty, so much sought after, became completely meaningless, and dependence of one man upon another was soon no more than the concomitant of the dependence of one estate upon another.[9]

The transformations in the meaning of the word 'family' reflect some of the changes in the nature of bondage, and the separation of certain protective functions from the household. But the wife's relationship to the husband was never a tie precisely of vassalage or serfdom:

> The wife only half belonged to the family in which her destiny placed her, perhaps not for very long. 'Be quiet', says Gavin le Lorain roughly to the widow of his murdered brother who is weeping over the body and bemoaning her lot, 'a noble knight will take you up again . . . it is I who must continue in deep mourning'.[10]

9. Marc Bloch, *Feudal Society*, Routledge & Kegan Paul, 1961, p. 236.
10. ibid., p. 136.

Moreover the wife retained her intimate connection to the immediate household; she remained in the physical presence of her lord long after the vassal had no such connection.

The resemblance between bonds within feudalism and the bond between man and woman in the family appears because social relations within the family mode of production are not directly on the cash-nexus. Female production for use means that women do not 'freely' sell their labour to men as a commodity. Yet it would be wrong to identify the relationship as feudal – the fact that it exists within capitalist society means that it is rather a component of the present stage of commodity production. Nor is it production for use as in a future communist society because the nature of what is useful is determined by the necessity of capitalism, not by the needs of human beings.

Because the particular division of labour which developed after the industrial revolution divided home from work, and removed the man from the home, leaving women who worked in the factories a double responsibility, the consciousness of women retained elements of the earlier forms of production. But ever since the nineteenth century friction has been very evident between the archaic forms which have not completely dissolved in the family and the pull of capitalist production. The emergence of rights for women indicates the weakening of the bond relationship between husband and wife. But this process is not yet complete.

Within capitalism women as workers in the family have not acquired characteristics Marx ascribed to workers in the commodity system. The worker encounters the owners of capital on the basis of equal rights and equality before the law. This is not yet the basis of relations between man and woman in marriage, despite significant improvements in women's rights in all the capitalist countries. Nor is there the same mobility of labour, though the relaxation in divorce laws is a development in this direction. Marx's distinction between the relationship of the 'free' worker and the worker in a relationship of bondage applies. 'If he were to sell it rump and stump, once and for all, he would be selling himself, converting himself from a free man into a slave, from an owner of a commodity into a commodity.'[11]

11. K. Marx, *Capital*, ed. D. Torr, Allen & Unwin, 1887, Vol. I, p. 146.

The woman in marriage has not yet become clearly dissociated from the property relationship which was much more apparent in the early stages of capitalism. It is still expressed, for instance, in the Lutheran hymn 'A safe stronghold our God is still', popular in the Methodist church. The hymn pledges trust in the Lord as the ultimate guardian who will not fail, 'And though they take our life, goods, honour, children, wife'. It still appears in the attitudes of country people on small-holdings where wives are close to being part of the means of production and a man has an eye for a good breeder because children are still stock and girls still fine fillies. On the small farm the household is still not completely separate from the place of production.

Although less immediately observable the notion of the wife as property, though a special form of property, is evident not only in the countryside now. Within the family the man appropriates the labour power of the woman in the exchange of services. Marriage contracts carry with them the connection between wives and goods and chattels. The man has the same kind of responsibility for care which went with them both in feudalism. He also has considerable freedom to mistreat his property. At the basis of the contract there is an inequality of social power which determines its terms. Marx's definition of property not as a substance or things but as a relationship is helpful. It implied '... man's attitude to his natural conditions of production as belonging to him as the prerequisites of himself which constitute as it were a prolongation of his body'.[12]

Ultimately the maintenance of this property relationship in which some human beings have become part of the property of another rests on superior force, economic, political, military, and ideological. Marx comments on the relationship between master and serf – 'What we have here as an essential relation of appropriation is the relationship of domination.'[13]

Thus not only does women's labour maintain a subordinate mode of production within capitalism, but women are generally

12. K. Marx, *Pre-Capitalist Economic Formations*, ed. E. J. Hobsbawm, Lawrence & Wishart, 1964, p. 89.

13. ibid., p. 102.

subordinate to men as a group within capitalist society. The consciousness of women reflects this subordination.

Because the family mode of production coexists within the dominant mode in a completely subordinate and dependent relation, the alternative notion of value which comes from it is as powerless to counter the dominant ideology of the commodity system as the family is to maintain itself in isolation from the production of commodities for exchange. The family now retains elements of earlier forms of production, but is still a creation of capitalism. An illustration of the total interdependence of the commodity system and the family is to be found in the precise fantasy of Spike Milligan's film *The Bedsitting Room.* After the atomic bomb falls commodity production is brought to a standstill. There are no goods, no market, no transport, a much-reduced demand. People are compelled to keep on moving around by the remains of the law which floats about in a big balloon. In this changed context the old relations persist but removed of all place and function appear as merely ludicrous and absurd. The lower-middle-class family continues to go round and round on the Circle Line, its privacy preserved in the carriage of a tube train, its snobbery satisfied by the suitability of the daughter's suitor who inhabits the carriage next door. Dad gets off regularly at the right station, but having no work to go to he sits on the platform and merely waits until the train comes round again. The daughter becomes pregnant by the boy next door. After they surface they continue to try and behave in roles which they believe to be socially correct for Mum, Dad, daughter and boy-friend, and amble about the atomic waste above in a bewildered but self-important manner, secure in their delusions of normality. But gradually in an abnormal reality, the 'normal' family disintegrates under the tension. The pregnancy goes on for eighteen months, Mum is seduced by a man who lives in a hole in the ground and who then vanishes. The family dissolves into cannibalism. Mum turns into a wardrobe in the bedsitting room where the daughter and boy-friend finally settle illegally. Dad becomes a parrot and is eaten for Sunday dinner. The destruction of the family when removed from the commodity system is complete.

Dependence of the family mode of production on the production of commodities means that the family can maintain or restrict the expansion of capital, but it cannot initiate change from itself. It is only by the transformation of social relations in the whole society that this subordination can be dissolved.

The family is the place where women work. It also determines the amount of labour which can be released for commodity production, and plays a crucial part in forming consciousness. The family is both essential for capital's reproduction, and a brake on its use of human labour power. The values of the family are both rational for the maintenance of the inhuman relations of commodity production, and irrational for a system of organizing the reproduction of human labour which is completely designed to produce commodities efficiently and has freed itself from all earlier property relations.

Women's liberation has been formed by the conflicting pressure of these antagonisms upon the life and social relations of women. This means we have a unique opportunity of attacking the consequences of capitalist society not only at the point of production, but also at the point of procreation.

Three questions are crucial for an understanding of the political implications of women's movement. What is the nature of women's production in the family and how is this reproduced in consciousness? How does the demand for women's labour in commodity production and the type of work women do in industry affect the consciousness of women? What are the ways in which capitalism is undermining the traditional contained sphere it has allotted to women since the industrial revolution, and what political consequences do these have?

These are huge questions and what follows is only the beginning of an answer.

CHAPTER 5

A Woman's Work is Never Done

Women are worse
than vessels,
holding broken
stems that only
children heal.

from Margo Magid, 'Birth Right',
Women, A Journal of Liberation,
Winter 1970

The irony behind the idyllic happy family as a place of repose is the consumption of female labour power. This labour remains unrecognized for the same reason as the worker's labour power is not given its true value. If it were admitted that the family is maintained at the expense of women, capitalism would have to devise some other way of getting the work done. Although this is not inconceivable, and housework could be socialized within capitalism, the political and social consequences as well as the economic cost would be considerable. At present it would seem to be more profitable for the capitalist system to continue to 'preserve the family'. Masculine cultural hegemony within capitalism has further blurred the issue. Work in capitalism is something men do. Men are the providers because they are paid money. Women are only allowed money by their husbands. Many men are suspicious of their wives achieving the status of wage-earner, because money – even a little money – means power and independence. Because housework does not fit into the prevailing notions of work it mysteriously becomes not work at all. It is not counted. The woman at home is described as a woman who doesn't work. 'In sheer quantity, household labour, including child care, constitutes a large amount of socially necessary production. Nevertheless, in a society based on commodity production, it is not usually considered "real work" since it is outside of trade and the market place.'[1]

One estimate of housewives' work showed housewives with children and without jobs doing an eighty-hour week, and women with children who went out to work doing an extra fifty hours at home every week.[2] Juliet Mitchell quotes other studies which also indicate something of the significance of this work which is not seen as work. 'Today it has been calculated in Sweden that 2,340 million hours a year are spent by women in housework compared with 1,290 million hours in industry. The Chase Manhattan Bank estimated a woman's overall working hours as averaging 99·6 per week.'[3]

The significance and value of female labour power has been obscured for all the same reasons that the labour of other subordinate groups is not given its due, but the peculiar nature of female oppression has made it particularly invisible. The fact that work outside the commodity system is not within the scope of economic calculation and that this work is done by women is part of the more general economic dominance and cultural hegemony of men over women. This can assume a personal psychological form in which some men are more contemptuous of women than others, but it is fundamentally a material relationship. Every individual man is forced to use his wife's expenditure of herself in the family in order to 'earn' money in the form of wages. He is dependent for his survival on her 'non-work' and is conditioned to see the world through male eyes and from the point of view of

1. Margaret Benston, 'The Political Economy of Women's Liberation', *Monthly Review*, New York, 1969.

2. Alain Girard, 'The Time Budget of Married Women in Urban Centres', in *Population*, 1968, quoted in Jean Gardiner, *The Economic Roots of Women's Liberation*, paper to International Socialism Conference on Women, June 1971.

3. Juliet Mitchell, *Women: The Longest Revolution*, New England Free Press, p. 7, see also Mitchell, *Woman's Estate*, Penguin, 1971.

the development and maintenance of male power. Although the working-class male or the black male are permitted an unequal share of this power, the male worker still receives the droppings of the ruling class to pad his wounded pride.

Nor is the connection of women to commodity production clear like that of the male worker: 'The labour of the worker and his wife is appropriated, the one directly, the other indirectly, by capital whilst only that portion of their labour time is paid (via the man) which is required to maintain them and perpetuate their labouring power at the customary standard of living established in the process of class struggle.'[4]

Within the process of class struggle there is a conflict between men and women which necessitates the reorganization of domestic as well as industrial work. Even if the means of production are socially owned and controlled, women remain part of the means of production for the individual man in the family. This has been disregarded by Marxists writing about women because the theory of surplus value, while relating clearly to the dominant capitalist mode of production, is difficult to apply to production within the family which is governed by quite different conditions and circumstances. Rather than straining Marx's categories of exploitation and surplus value, worked out to explain commodity production, into the family mode of production and quibbling about the use of oppression and exploitation in this context, we have to analyse women's labour in the home on its own terms and develop new concepts. At this stage we really only have moral descriptions of long hours; except for the crude recognition of its necessity to commodity production, we have no means of measuring labour time consumed in housework in social terms. The construction of such an analysis is an important part of the tasks of women's liberation.

The non-recognition of women's labour in the home leaves them with no sense of value as a group at all. The subordination of women as a group and the particular nature of female conditioning serve to maintain this. So while women can morally assert their worth, and resist the reduction of their value to the

4. Jean Gardiner, *The Economic Roots of Women's Liberation*, paper to International Socialism Conference on Women, June 1971.

lowest estimate of commodity exchange, as for example in a case in which a judge rated women's value at 50p an hour when awarding a man damages for the death of his wife in a car accident, this remains merely defensive. One woman commented for instance to an *Evening Standard* reporter, 'It's typical of this horrible materialistic society putting everything down to £ s. d. You cannot put a price on a wife. You've got to be a psychologist, a nurse, a laundress, a maid-of-all-work and everything. I never stop, usually washing the floor after midnight . . . High Court judges, they can afford au pair girls.'[5]

Such a consciousness can resist devaluation but it can't transform the circumstances in which women are reduced to 50p an hour, or the notion of measuring the value of human beings by the money rate of their labour. It can never break to the surface and unite in a theory which can become a point around which to organize. Ultimately the only way of establishing an alternative value of female human beings is to shatter the system of capitalist production at home as well as at work. Only when the notion of human value can become general in a society without exploitation can both the relationship between man and woman and the relationship of human beings to nature cease to be relations determined by the needs of commodity production.

Housework is not only excluded from the prevailing economic notion of value, the actual nature of the work makes it invisible in another sense. Men do not generally see it being done. The woman in the home works in isolation while the man is away. When he returns he notices absences, things which have not been done. The day's routine of tasks is not apparent because they result merely in the creation of a normal environment for him. Only the woman and perhaps the children look at a room and remember its transformations through the day. But housework often does not seem like job work even to the women. It is very different from work outside. Obviously there is no wage, no union, no strike. There is no clear distinction between work place and leisure, no clocking in and out, no time-and-motion study. It stretches over the whole time of existence broken only by illness and holidays. Its space is the whole space of a woman's life. A

5. *Evening Standard*, 3 Feb. 1971.

woman does not go to work, she wakes up to work. Home is work and work is home. Within the space of the house and the time of the day there are certain tasks to be done. The tasks are the boundaries of a woman's work in the home. Each operation is broken up into small parts. Each one is quite distinct and separate. Get up, breakfast, wash up, make the beds, dress the children, take them to school, come back, cleaning, polishing, wiping, shopping, make lunch, collect children, wash up, take children back, sort things out, washing, prepare tea, husband comes home, eat, wash up, watch television, put the children to bed, make some coffee, watch television, talk to husband, go to bed, make love. The day is carefully delineated, the operations are repeated again and again but the context changes every day. The whole series of tasks present themselves within a new total situation. So every day is the same and yet not the same and sucks you into itself as a person rather than a 'worker'.

The maintenance and surpassing of the work routine is a constant effort. The housewife tries to save time, she tries to accumulate space and time in order to push out the boundaries so she can have a little 'time to herself'. The attempt disintegrates continuously. She is only safe in the bath. A complex of forces prevent her from ever getting ahead of herself. One big spurt and the floor gleams, one achievement, so much labour power consumed in one task, and proportionally less left over for all the rest. The achievement itself disappears almost as it is accomplished. Children with dirty shoes they forget to wipe come home from school – one dirty floor.

An endless routine, it creates its own high moments of achievement and satisfaction so as to evade not monotony – the feature of many jobs – but futility. The bolt you tighten on the factory floor vanishes to be replaced by another; but the clean kitchen floor is tomorrow's dirty floor and the clean floor of the day after that. The appropriate symbol for housework ... is not the interminable conveyor belt but a compulsive circle like a pet mouse in its cage spinning round on its exercise wheel, unable to get off. Into this one inserts one's own saving peaks: 'Happiness is the bathroom scrubbed down.' But even the glorious end of today's chores is not even an anti-climax as there is no real climax – there is nothing to fill 'the joyful moment'. But the routine is never quite routine, so the vacuum in one's mind is never vacuous enough to be filled. 'Housework is a worm eating away at one's ideas.' Like a fever dream it goes on and on until you desperately hope that it can be achieved at one blow. You lay the breakfast the night before, you have even been known to light the gas under the kettle for tomorrow's tea, wishing that by breakfast time everything could be over with by 8 a.m., the children washed, teeth cleaned and ready for bed: tucked up, *the end.*[6]

Housework devours itself, there is a kind of cyclical rhythm of endeavour and collapse – into exhaustion. There is a peculiar kind of exhaustion in work which half-preoccupies you – fatigue!

In industry the most fatiguing jobs are those which only partially occupy the worker's attention, but at the same time prevent him from concentrating on anything else. Many young wives say that this mental grey-out is what bothers them most in caring for home and children. 'After a while your mind becomes a blank,' they say. 'You can't concentrate on anything. It's like sleep-walking . . .' Since the demands of housework and child-rearing are not very flexible, there is no complete solution to chronic-fatigue problems. Many women, however, can cut down fatigue if they stop asking too much of themselves. By trying to understand realistically what she can – and, most important, what she cannot – do, a woman may, in the long run, be a better wife and mother, albeit a tired one.[7]

This ignores that the straining to get beyond the boundaries of the day's tasks is essential in terms of morale. Once you stop straining, the deadening quality of what you are doing overwhelms you. The routine in fact can rarely be overtaken by the woman's efforts, partly because housework is not just effort but continuity as well, and also because the infinitely variable needs of children and husbands determine the structure of the job.

When the housework was still new, I used to take a little pleasure in finding ways of doing the jobs quicker and better. But it is an exhaustible subject of interest. Now I am simply bent on eliminating

6. Paper given by Peckham Women's Liberation Workshop at Women's Liberation Conference, Oxford, February 1970, printed in *A Woman's Work is Never Done*, Agitprop, London.

7. 'Why Young Mothers are Always Tired', *Redbook*, Sept 1959, quoted in Friedan, *The Feminine Mystique*, p. 220.

as many tasks as possible. This is sensible to a certain extent. Joe did not notice the sheets are unironed last week, so it seems pointless to iron them any more – but it does cut the ground from under my feet. Another factor that undermines my interest is having to keep my mind on two things at once. I used to get very tense carrying on with a task while making sure Carl was not getting into trouble. I have overcome that by freeing the surface of my mind from thoughts altogether, leaving it swimming aimlessly so that it can be called into action by an alarming sound. This is a further loosening of concentration and one that has to be practised for a distressingly large part of the day, often leaving me too empty for real concentration when the chance comes. And as I said, any inclination I might have to take my work seriously is comically scotched by Carl himself, in his constructive moments as much as his destructive ones. Anything I do attracts his attention, so if I tidy a room he picks up the object as I put it down. Or if I clean windows on his level he comes after me, imitating my movements with his hands, and smearing what I have just done. Even if I give him a duster his fingers slip off; it is the movement he is intent on, not the sense of the gesture. I begin to feel hilariously unreal.[8]

The activity of housework, the cleaning and tidying and cooking, is interwoven with the work which relates directly to human beings. Housework can never be a normal job routine because emotion erupts in its midst. Crisis and turmoil mean that the woman has to drop everything and put Humpty together again. Friends phone, children run home screaming, the husband glowers behind his paper, the woman retreats behind a barrier of elaborate calm. Brought up to feel she must keep things going, patch and cover up, settle everyone down, she absorbs the tension magically within herself until it is no longer evident. The original barrier becomes a case between her and the world, the case hardens, the violence she has contained ravages her. She begins to feel completely hollow.

It was never a burden to me to be a woman before I had Carl. Feminists had seemed to me to be tilting at windmills; women who allowed men to rule them did so from their own free choice. I felt that

8. Suzanne Gail, 'The Housewife', in *Work*, ed. Ronald Fraser, Penguin, 1968, pp. 149–50.

I had proved myself the intellectual equal of men, and maintained my femininity as well. But afterwards I quite lost my sense of identity; for weeks it was an effort to speak. And when I again became conscious of myself as other than a thing, it was in a state of rebellion which I had to clamp down firmly because of Carl. I also grew very thin and I still do not menstruate.[9]

In a society which values people by the wages they earn women receive no wage and do work which is barely recognized as work, in which productivity can't be measured and nothing is ever ultimately accomplished. They do this in a society which conditions women to believe they are inferior to men, that women were brought into the world to magnify a man's image of himself and serve him. Not surprisingly women sometimes feel as if they carried round a void inside them. One day when she was pregnant my next-door neighbour wandered in and said, 'We women are just shells for the men.' When you sink your identity into someone else you suddenly get a terrifying feeling that you are no longer there.

When I am by myself, I am nothing. I only know that I exist because I am needed by someone who is real, my husband, and by my children. My husband goes out into the real world. Other people recognize him as real, and take him into account. He affects other people and events. He does things and changes things, which are different afterwards. I stay in his imaginary world in this house, doing jobs that I largely invent, and that no one cares about but myself. I do not change things. The work I do changes nothing; what I cook disappears, what I clean one day must be cleaned again the next. I seem to be involved in some sort of mysterious process rather than actions that have results.

The only time that I think I might be real in myself is when I hear myself screaming or having hysterics. But it is at these times that I am in the most danger . . . of being told that I am wrong, or that I'm not really like what I'm acting like, or that he hates me. If he stops loving me, I'm sunk; I won't have any purpose in life, or be sure I exist any more. I must efface myself in order to avoid this and not make any demands on him, or do anything that might offend him. I feel dead now, but if he stops loving me I am really dead, because I

9. ibid., p. 146.

am nothing by myself. I have to be noticed to know I exist. But if I efface myself, how can I be noticed? It is a basic contradiction.[10]

Women have devised particular resistances within the framework of their lives as they are. There is the switching-off, the half-there swimmy feeling, the barriers round yourself, and there is illness. Fatigue, hysteria, nervous complaints, agoraphobia. Tranquillizers, sleeping pills and supermarket alcohol are the remedies. The relationship between bad housing conditions, a low standard of living and a woman's health is obvious – anaemia, headaches, constipation, rheumatism, gynaecological trouble, varicose veins, ulcerated legs, phlebitis, obesity. There are psychological as well as physical symptoms of poverty. A wife of an unemployed man in Essex during the Depression in the 1930s described its effect.

The constant struggle with poverty this last four years has made me feel very nervy and irritable and this affects my children. I fear I have not the patience that good health generally brings. When I am especially worried about anything I feel as if I have been engaged in some terrific physical struggle and go utterly limp and for some time am unable to move or even think coherently. This effect of mental strain expressed in physical results seems most curious and I am at a loss to properly explain it to a doctor.[11]

This is in the thirties but it would be naïve to imagine that poverty has vanished in the 1970s. It still assumes its old forms but it has also acquired new ones. You may find a place in which to live that isn't damp, with no holes behind the wallpaper and with hot water, but it could be on top of a tower block so that the children can't get out. This new kind of poverty produces its own pathology. A recent study of mental health in tower blocks has revealed an exceptionally high incidence of neurosis. Enough indeed to produce an advertising campaign for tranquillizers. A medical journal, *The Practitioner*, has been carrying an advert for the drug Serenid-D produced by John Wyeth Ltd. There was a picture of a young mother with a pram in front of a big block of

10. Meredith Tax, *Woman and Her Mind, The Story of Daily Life*, a Bread and Roses Publication, 1970, p. 7.
11. Margery Spring Rice, *Working Class Wives*, Penguin, 1939, p. 69.

flats and the heading, 'She can't change her environment but you can change her mood with Serenid-D.' The advertisement added blandly that 'neurotic illness has been shown to occur with greater frequency in women flat dwellers' and was becoming an increasing problem to 'the community at large'.

However, there are illnesses which have nothing to do with poverty, which come simply from being housebound and being a woman in capitalist society. A Boston analyst told Betty Friedan there were far more women patients than men. 'Their complaints are varied, but if you look underneath you find this underlying feeling of emptiness. It is not inferiority, it is almost like nothingness. The situation is that they are not pursuing any goals of their their own.'[12]

The neurosis of nothingness comes directly from the nature of women's work in the home. Self-affirmation can only come through self-abnegation. The 'feminine' woman, the good mother, can only realize herself by pouring herself into her husband and children. She has to give herself in service and find herself through other people and through the objects around her in the house.

> In the home the woman is *in the family* and the two are disturbingly synonymous. Housework cannot be separated from children, nor the children from the four walls, the food you cook, the shopping you do, the clothes you wear. How you, the house, the children, *look* may not be how they are, but reflects what you want them to be. It is not just that every pop psychologist's 'mum' lives in a *Woman's Own* dream house, where the material solution to every problem is immediately at hand, it is that in our society being a mother is being a housewife: the security of the family is the stability of the walls. The image of the family home is the image of the family.[13]

When you go out to work the job is something you *do*. But the work of a housewife and mother is not just something you do, it's somebody you are. Because women's work in the home retains certain pre-capitalist elements, the bonds of the family are not on the cash-nexus; the work-discipline and wage-time of the factory

12. Friedan, op. cit., p. 256.
13. Peckham Women's Liberation Workshop, op. cit., p. 5.

don't exist; the things women make are consumed more or less immediately, a woman is not transformed into a hand or an operator. Quite the contrary, women's work is completely unspecialized. A woman in one day performs the functions of innumerable workers, dustbin man, nurse, cleaner, psychiatrist, stripper, fortune-teller, cook. A woman has to be all kinds of people on demand. She has the satisfaction of knowing she is working for people she cares for. From the outside she appears freer than a man working for someone else and without any affection in his job. But because this caring work goes on in the context of a society where work is predominantly divorced from care, because she is isolated in the home, bearing the load of all the sentiment which is out of place in the man's work, and because of the division of labour which relegates caring to women and brands women as inferior, distortion is inevitable. If care were truly social, there would be no need for defensive homes as castles, tenderness would not be connected with submission, nor love with possession. It is not surprising that violence breaks out in the family, or that people are made victims of families, that children are devoured, and smothered and hurt and battered in families. The family under capitalism carries an intolerable weight: all the rags and bones and bits of old iron the capitalist commodity system can't use. Within the family women are carrying the preposterous contradiction of love in a loveless world. They are providing capitalism with the human relations it cannot maintain in the world of men's work. Within this framework women are subordinate to men but are allowed a peculiar kind of respect as long as they fulfil their 'role'.

The complex sexual conditioning of little girls of all classes, the social education into femininity and domesticity, has broken us into submitting to this. The whole paraphernalia of not competing with men, of becoming stupid when confronted with machines or ideas, our delicacy, our incompetence, our softness, our capacity for boring, monotonous work, our masochism, our hysteria, emotionalism, sentimentality have no more a mysterious source than the 'ignorance' of workers, the cheerfulness of the 'naturally' grinning 'nigger'. They serve the same 'useful' economic function of making groups who lack power and control within capitalism accept this state of affairs with the minimum of resistance. But whereas crime and violence are common responses from men who are oppressed, the particular form of female conditioning produces neurosis rather than 'criminality'.

Like other groups which are subordinate in society women have however also devised their own strategies to maintain an alternative myth of self-respect. This never achieves the hegemonic quality of the ideology of the dominant group. It has always a fragmented and incomplete character. But it serves to give the oppressed a limited notion of their own intelligibility. It establishes for them a place in the world, even if the place is not one they would have chosen for themselves. When the work you do appears meaningless, when the routine that surrounds you is out of your control, you clear private spaces, charter your own routes round apparently impassable boundaries. The experienced housewife is no exception. Private space is always disguised as an activity. Having a bath is one. Carefully inefficient shopping is another. Rationally it is absurd when women keep nipping out to the shops – shopping time could be considerably reduced. But as a strategy for breaking down the isolation of the nuclear family, and the barriers of the home, it makes personal sense. Making work for yourself is another way of clearing a path through your surroundings. Women who do this assert their own notion of their value in defiance of the dominant male sense of value. But they never challenge the idea of work in the commodity system head on. They merely wear themselves out with a labour that values itself on the basis of its never-ending, masochistic character and subsists within the dominant cash system. Housework is communicated as a craft and mothers condition young girls into its mysteries. Cleanliness and shine assume a fetishistic quality for the houseproud woman. It is almost as if she seeks her own reflection desperately in the surfaces she polishes.

The origins of this pride in the job, so near to neurosis, often come from a very practical situation. If you're living in cramped, bad housing without a bath and hot water, and your husband comes in dirty and tired from work, the things you have to do to make life tolerable duplicate themselves. You simply can't afford to leave any tasks half-finished. You have to be extra-careful to complete every little job. Otherwise they quickly accumulate into twice as much clearing up later. You also get demoralized much quicker. Stoning the outdoor steps, endless lino polishing, the washing of lace curtains, have their own rationale when your estate is a back to back. It is the woman's contribution to maintaining the family's self-respect. Such habits die hard. Long after the old necessity has gone women work according to the old routine. A young mother in a flat or even one room becomes flat- or room-bound with childbirth. 'Her helpless child is her jailor. Its total dependence is its total power, it dictates her moods by its moods.'[14] Even after the child has grown older she will continue to live within the former confines of her family. She is rather like those mental patients and prisoners who are terrified to live without the safe and known routine of their institution. This is our own kind of 'institutionalization'.

Women recognize that their role is intolerable so they switch off their minds and make themselves believe that the trivial chores are of great importance. They exist by concentrating on the rituals of housework (in the case of houseproud women the ritual has become a religion), in this way a woman can block out the realities of her hopeless situation and simply cope with her existence.[15]

Indeed in the apparently pointless toil the houseproud woman finds her own sense of worth.

In a desperate search for recognition of her drudgery a woman may begin to delight in the fantasy that 'my husband could never cope on his own', and 'my child would never go to anyone else', and 'no one can get his shirts up like I can'. Obviously it is in the man's and children's self-interest not to shatter the illusion. To compensate her lack of purpose she has to nurture the image of the indispensable housewife who devotes her life to her husband and children. The prison she calls a home, at first imposed on her by motherhood, or rather society's solution to the care of pre-school children, has become the only proof of years of sacrifice and is almost sacred in her eyes. Even when she openly recognizes the sacrifice, she tends to see it as martyrdom and is proud to have 'given her life' for her family.[16]

14. Mavis Redfern, 'Contact', in *Shrew*, October 1970.
15. ibid.
16. ibid.

Housework creates its own culture and is communicated collectively.

Whilst it is generally true that housewives talk of nothing but housework, babies and other women, I do not think that it is only (though probably primarily) because they have nothing else to talk about. I feel that she needs to discover how her fellow 'workers' manage in order to assess her own value, and in her turn pass on information of her own household achievements to others.[17]

The woman who becomes obsessive about housework seeks her own sense of value. By constantly tidying up she proves that she is needed. This can turn into a kind of power which traps husband and children, and makes them see home as their prison too. But it is important to recognize what kind of value women find in housework. Every time housework is devalued women who are bound up with their homes feel threatened. Simply going out to work can help but it is not enough because all women are so deeply conditioned to find their own reflections and image in their family and home. Audrey Wise, an active trade unionist in USDAW, the shop workers' union, told me, 'Even women who now make an economic contribution to the home retain to a large extent the feeling that it is their work at home which makes them indispensable. Over and over I have heard women describe how they must go on working at home until everything is perfect, even after they have done a full day's employment, and even though their husbands often say, "Leave it, you've done enough".'

The psychological bondage remains even after its economic rationale has dissolved.

17. Mavis Redfern, 'Contact', in *Shrew*, October 1970.

CHAPTER 6

Sitting Next to Nellie

Whether it was the old story of 'sitting next to Nellie' to learn the job; whether it was going through the factory training school, so-called, since for women the factory school was never anything but just a speeding-up lane leading to just another repetitious job at piece work speed; whether it was attending the Government Training Centre to learn a skilled job as a wartime dilutee, whether it was going to night school to rustle up the necessary maths to do the job; whether it was getting put back in the unskilled female labour category, after the war, and sitting next to Nellie again, I have shared the experiences of many.

Mrs. H. Sloane, National Union of
General and Municipal Workers,
T.U.C. Congress 1968

I was threatened with the sack for saying five words. That means that anybody could get it at any time. Nobody is going to answer him back at all now, just for fear of losing their job. My friend has six kids and her husband is sick. Most of the women want to keep the job because of buying little extras and for a decent standard of living. Some of us really need the job because of hardship and responsibilities at home. We are all scared of losing it and he knows it . . .

After a few years of it you shut up and get on with the job.

'Conditions in a Northern Factory as
Described to Me by My Mother',
Shrew, June 1971, p. 4

Going out to work has represented for middle-class women the hope of freedom. There is a strong tradition in feminism which sees a job as an answer to women identifying with their home, children, and husband. Demands for better opportunities for women to work in the commodity system have been an important part of feminist programmes. Among the left generally the notion of equal rights extends to better training for working-class women and the chance for women to become skilled. Marxists have supported women's working so that they could acquire understanding of industrial organization and class solidarity. Action around production rather than procreation has been the only kind of militancy imaginable. Sometimes it works out like this. Some older women trade unionists do achieve such a political consciousness. But they are very much in a minority. Other women at work do arrive at an independence and a mateyness and don't get so obsessed with whether or not the house is clean. A woman who used to live in a flat above me would talk of how she wished she could work part time in the factory she'd been in before she'd had children, just for the company. Having money that's really your own is important too because it means you have the right to tell a man where he can get off.

But simply working in commodity production isn't going to free women, because it is still determined by the essential production women are responsible for in the family. If capitalism were to effect a complete transformation in the way this family work is organized and in the complicated conditioning of women which makes them accept housework, only then could women really be involved in production. Although such a change is not completely inconceivable, the economic and social cost would mean a capitalism which was fundamentally different from any system known now and would probably be extremely destructive to its own continuation. The room we have for manoeuvre is very strictly limited by the changes produced by the pursuit of profit. But although we are confined in our everyday agitation, within the limits capitalism imposes on us we have to try to turn events to our advantage, and take new tendencies in the direction of our interests.

In the case of women's work there is an undeniable contradiction. At one side women's work in the family remains essential. Indeed the more the family contracts in size the louder the volume of noise about the importance of its preservation. Conservative members of the ruling class exalt the woman who stays at home partly because this is the cheapest way of maintaining commodity producers, partly because the ideology of woman's 'place' and the consolation of 'no place like home' help to keep them secure. Yet the expansion of production means there are goods to sell and new kinds of jobs to be done. The reduction of housework time, which the penetration of consumer goods makes possible if not always actually realizable, combined with contraception and early marriage, has meant that many more married women have been 'released' for commodity production. Increased productivity involves the tapping of new sources of labour power. Since the 1930s the absorption of married women on the labour market has been on a scale comparable to the initial absorption of agricultural labour into the early factories. Woman-power has thus become increasingly an integral and essential part of commodity production. By making use of both husband's and wife's labour capitalism has been able to allow the family unit a higher income. The rise in the rate of exploitation of the family has only tardily led to any change in the organization of work in the family. Most women have been left with a double load. In Britain, for example, nursery facilities have been drastically cut since the war. However, in America recently progressive capitalists have been arguing for such facilities on the grounds that women won't be able to give their best in commodity production without alternative provision for the children. This is consistent but expensive – and capitalism even at the peaks of its prosperity is notoriously mean and money-grubbing.

The use of the labour of married women in advanced capitalism is part of complicated changes in the structure and organization of work, as well as the need always to find new markets and to effect continual changes in the nature of demand. Despite the dependence of capitalism now on married women as a permanent and essential part of the work force employers are still apt to behave as if they were doing women a favour by employing them. They still act as if women should somehow be grateful for the chance to be exploited. This is particularly ironic in view of the actual nature of the jobs which are categorized as 'women's work'. The only factor these jobs really have in common is low pay, which means the profit capitalism takes from women is direct and crude. The cheap labour of women is an alternative to investing in machinery.

Originally 'women's work' was an extension of the household. Tasks which related to production in the home remained women's when work and home became separated. Despite many changes some industries retain this. Textile and clothing still have a large female labour force in Britain, although because of overall decline and the introduction of new machinery there are actually fewer skilled women employed. Food production and catering are also largely done by women.

The process of mechanization in the industrial revolution broke up craft skills and devalued particular work operations and often led to women replacing men. Now these developments continue and as a result of both technological change and of rationalization of the work process operations have been reduced down to their simplest parts. This creates the need to redefine skills and tends to produce new forms of differentiation between workers. In a study of the French metal industry Madeleine Guilbert shows how automation has decreased the number of women employed both by replacing them by machines and substituting men for women when the machines needed care and attention.[1] Employers persistently believe that women are incapable of being trained to look after new and complex machinery. At the same time automation has strengthened the segregation between men and women. Because women's work in industry has come to be seen as short-cycle operations with one gesture strictly identical to the other, women are most threatened by automation, are paid less, and a sociological literature has flourished proving women are 'naturally' suited to routine, boring and monotonous work, although it has also been shown that women's commitment to their work is directly related to the skill involved and their training levels. Indeed for the word 'natural' in relation to women workers it is always sensible to read either 'conditioned' or 'profitable'. For example, Madeleine Guilbert points out that speed and dexterity, which are regarded as a

1. Madeleine Guilbert, *Les Fonctions des femmes dans l'industrie*, Paris, 1966, pp. 223–7.

specific natural aptitude of women – but not paid for in higher wages – in fact repeat the use of arms and hands in housework. Tasks like cooking and sewing require a deft coordination of movements which can be used in industry.[2]

But because the concept of 'woman's work' is only spuriously rational and is in reality rather a justification for the existing inequality of social power between men and women, so called 'natural' female aptitudes aren't 'valued' in money terms, although other factors such as physical weakness are subtracted from the 'value' of female workers in industry. Even here there are exceptions – women do work which is both dirty and physically tiring when it appears as an extension of housework. Indeed the more closely work resembles housework the less it has the status of 'real' work. Cleaning is a clear example of this.[3] The low pay of cleaners, both in offices and factories, represents the money value capitalism puts on housework when it appears within the commodity system. Cleaning is increasingly coming under a system of contract labour and involves all the usual inequities of such a system. Completely outside the Factory Acts, with very little capital equipment and soaring profits, it provides an ideal opportunity for contractors to extract labour from the cleaners, not only by normal industrial practices but by a host of petty tricks and fiddles. Nobody checks if the numbers of women specified on a contract are actually in a building, so a very small group of women find themselves covering for others and doing more and more floors. Night cleaning work is stretched over the night from 10 p.m. until the first transport so even if there is only a small group of women they are stuck with one building to clean. This is like cleaning a house but magnified to grotesque proportions. It is also much dirtier. Wages for night cleaning are low, around £14; evening cleaning means shorter hours and proportionally less money.

Many of the women doing cleaning are forced into it, either because they have no other training, or because they are too old to get other work. Sometimes it's because they have large families

2. ibid., p. 214.

3. See *The Night Cleaners' Special*, Socialist Woman pamphlet, and 'The Night Cleaners' Special Issue', *Shrew*, December 1971.

and have nowhere to put their young children during the day, so lack of nursery facilities forces them to work at night. During the day they are left with their children and can get very little sleep, locking themselves in the bedroom so the children don't get hurt. Many are widows or unsupported mothers who have to bring up their families alone. A Prices and Incomes Board report published in April 1971 showed that a quarter of the women surveyed were the sole providers for their families. Also about one fifth were from families with an income below £14 per week, and more than 3 per cent were living on the poverty line.

Cleaning retains the isolation of housework. At night the City of London is a lonely and desolate place and the tiny groups of cleaners are lost in the vast buildings. All night workers are forgotten and neglected people. It is almost as if they didn't exist. They are shuffled out of the way of daytime capitalism, emerging only on the first tubes and buses with that special pallor characteristic of people who don't see much of the light. But even when they are physically visible in hospitals, for example, cleaners still have a strangely subterranean existence. A ward maid at the Royal Free Hospital describes the life of the lowest grade of workers in the hospital as 'an underground labyrinth of corridors and workshops, drains and cockroaches'.[4]

But at the same time cleaning in a large institution has elements of the regimentation of factory work. Although cleaners in a hospital are expected to clean without being seen, they have their own world within the hospital world and their own underground routine. 'Every minute you move is on a long list. You take the woolly wash from the fourth floor every morning and you have ten minutes to get it downstairs. At twenty past ten you take the tea things out of the steriliser. It's boiling hot and it burns your fingers.'[5]

Many immigrant women clean because they face all the normal disadvantages of women at work combined with racial discrimination. Within capitalism the weakest go under and stay under, so immigrant women – Cypriot, West Indian, Italian, Spanish,

4. 'Lower Depths', in *Germ's Eye View* (London), no. 2, Summer 1970.
5. 'Barbara Talking', *Shrew*, October 1970.

Irish – are among the worst-paid workers. Along with women who have become individual casualties, unmarried mothers, widows, older women, immigrant women tend to be concentrated together in the most unpleasant jobs. Capitalism creates ghettos in industry as well as in towns.

There are no indications that within the capitalist organization of production any egalitarian tendency can be observed. What has happened is a change in the structure of particular industries, a process of expansion and contraction by which some workers have been displaced and others taken on in different sectors. The historical course of this movement and the consequences for women remain unexplored. But certain obvious features are apparent. While technological change eliminates certain types of women's work, it throws up the need for other kinds of jobs. In the last twenty years in Britain and America the tendency for married women workers to be integrated increasingly within the commodity system has had important effects. Women have not been used to displace male workers or to compensate for a shortage of labour, but have become important contributors to the family income because new kinds of work have developed. This means their working life is more continuous and they are likely to have a more permanent consciousness as wage-earners. It also means that they have more independence in relation to men at home. Until the 1930s domestic service meant that many women were performing their traditional domestic role in isolated home units, some even living in. The decline of the large household with servants and the opening-up of new work has made important changes in the female job structure. This expansion has been largely because of the growth in the service sector and in unskilled clerical work. However, in the context of this expansion the traditional features of 'women's work' have reproduced themselves. Women are at the bottom, the work is an extension of familial roles, hard work appears disguised, and the pay is low. For example, in America the number of women in sales work has grown particularly rapidly:

Since 1950, there has been a 30% increase in the number of women employed in this field, and they now constitute 42% of all sales workers, 58% of all retail sales workers. Women in sales work tend to be concentrated in salaried jobs, often at minimum wage or below, while the high commission sales jobs, such as in appliances or autos, are reserved for men. Women also make up the vast bulk of cashiers – again, at minimum wage or below with no commissions. Furthermore, over 50% of all women in sales are part-time or temporary workers, a percentage exceeded only by household workers.[6]

The changing structure of distribution with the growth of supermarkets has altered the character of shop work but because serving in a shop fits the traditional notions of work suitable for women this is completely ignored. For instance, many girls in supermarkets are shelf-fillers.

You lift a box of goods, say tinned soup, on to a table. The carton will probably have two layers. You slit it open, stamp each tin with the price and load the half cartons on to a trolley. When full (and I mean full) you wheel it to a lift and take it down from the stock room to the store-room. The stock room is quiet and a bit dim ... There is no chatter. The store is very brightly lit, and probably there is Muzak. The whole atmosphere is different and rather disorientating. You then unload your trolley in the appropriate place, then proceed back to the stock room. You have virtually no contact with customers. You are what in a factory is often called a 'Materials Handler', i.e. a labourer. But in a factory you would have Saturdays off. Here you work most Saturdays and probably till 8 on Fridays.[7]

As long as work resembles housework the fact that it is heavy doesn't matter. Other aspects of women's role in the family are also utilized by the commodity system in capitalism. In Britain approximately 40 per cent of all girls leaving school now go into clerical work. Again their chance of reaching the upper grades is minimal and the increasing mechanization of offices is affecting the nature of the work.[8] Before the introduction of the typewriter

6. Irene Winkler, *Women Workers: The Forgotten Third of the Working Class*, U S International Socialism pamphlet.

7. Letter from Audrey Wise, member of the Union of Shop, Distributive and Allied Workers (U S D A W), May 1971.

8. Nancy Seear, *The Position of Women in Industry*, H M S O, 1968, pp. 2, 7.

secretarial and clerical work was masculine and regarded as unsuitable for females. Mechanization made it women's work. In the twenties in America the 'White Collar Girl' became a popular theme in novels, girls like Una Golden in Sinclair Lewis's *The Job* were thrown onto the labour market and out of the middle class. For the working-class girl the typewriter also represented a way up. The office has produced its own hierarchies, a particularly delicate snobbishness between private secretary and typing pool. The photocopying machine has reduced the amount of typing. Now the secretary is attached to the telephone instead. There are often long spaces between work. But the protection of the boss has become more demanding. A feminine aide is a kind of status symbol to reassure the executive of his importance.

Advice to secretaries is always about self-presentation – how to leave the room, where to do your nails. In fact the women in the office are essential to the preservation of the firm. Their appearance is all-important. 'She *is* the office,' write the editors of *Fortune*. 'The male is the name on the door, the hat on the hat rack, and the smoke in the corner room. But the male is not the office.'[9]

Thus the woman in the office transposes the task of the woman in the home into the wage sector. Amongst older women a trim motherly manner is cultivated, for the younger girls a certain contained sexuality is demanded as part of the job. 'Always look beautiful but not provocative,' urges the *Sunday Times*.[10] Baby has to be hot enough for manpower but not too hot to distract him from the 'serious' work of making money. Female sexuality in the office is calculated in relation to productivity. Robert Nolan, vice-president of a Kentucky management consultancy, is reported as saying, 'Ideally offices that put productivity over frivolity should ban both the mini and hot pants and insist on more moderate fashions – such as knee-length skirts or even slacks.' He qualified this however with the information that hot pants don't interrupt efficiency as much as minis because the 'anticipatory time is cut down'. Men know they can take every-

9. Quoted in C. Wright Mills, *White Collar*, New York, 1956, p. 200.
10. Quoted in Germaine Greer, *The Female Eunuch*, Paladin, 1970, p. 124.

thing in with a quick glance because they won't see anything more when the girl 'stoops to open a file'.[11]

Female conditioning into self-denying service means that women even with relatively high earnings drop into looking after men. Germaine Greer describes how the Alfred Marks Bureau in London found that 80 per cent of secretaries earning more than £1000 a year were prepared to run errands for their bosses, 74 per cent would do his shopping, 73 per cent would lie to protect him. You can see this everywhere, not just in offices. Girls in hairdressers also run errands for the man in charge. A friend of mine who was a dental receptionist used to wash the dentist's shirts. All this is not because women are a peculiar breed of mugs, but because by doing these tasks which are expected of them women at work are subtly flattered that their sex is recognized. This makes them feel that they are not quite on the cash-nexus, that they matter to their employer in the same way that they matter to men in their personal lives. Male employers often use sex to control women and maintain their authority at the work place. This divides the work force and makes it very difficult to organize. Older men can come over in a fatherly way.

Thus the notion of woman's work as an extension of woman's role in the family serves to conceal that much of this work is hard and dirty; it also enables employers to retain paternalistic forms of control over women workers and extract more labour power from them which does not even find reflection in the wage packet.

The expansion in higher education, the growth of state intervention in the socialization of the work force, have provided the other significant changes in the structure of women's employment. Women's liberation developed first at the most highly developed point of capitalist society, the production of a new kind of intellectual skilled worker in mass higher and further education. The apparently sexless equality of the student world is illusory. The clash between home values and university or college is extreme for all students from families where higher

11. 'Memo to a Boss: Hot Pants beat the Mini', in the *Daily Mirror*, 2 April 1971.

education is unfamiliar. This is especially true for female students. Girls who go to university encounter capitalism in one of its most sophisticated forms, but their socialization in the family has prepared them for marriage and motherhood, traditional production at home. Temporarily co-workers with boys in the knowledge industry, the contrast between their traditional feminine role and competitive academic life is extreme. The gap between liberal educational promise and future occupational reality is even wider too for them than the boys. It was not that the post-war generation were the first to experience this, but they were the first women to reach higher education in large numbers who did not belong to a privileged elite.

The way in which these female knowledge workers are absorbed into production means that they continue to be aware of their contradictory social position. This is true both of their position and of their function. The predominance of women in the lower grades of teaching and social work is no coincidence. These are capitalism's 'soft' institutions and again women are presenting capitalism's human face in labour – increasingly part of the task of policing the unruly and delinquent. Women are the soft cops who bring you a cup of tea after the hard men have done you over.

Charity work on the cash-nexus is extremely important in making capitalism appear less personally intransigent. It's the sugar on the pill, the patching on the worn-out quilt. Welfare measures and education are obviously essential gains of working-class agitation, social work and teaching are necessary and useful jobs amidst the devastation capitalism creates. But in our society they serve a dual function, of straightforward help and of social and political containment. Ironically women are ideally suited by their conditioning to help and to contain. However, as they become critical of their own socialization they become increasingly aware of the contradictory nature of their jobs and continually conscious of failure, because success within the context of the work often means a kind of domestication of rebellion and the breaking of hopeless defiance.

Teaching and social work alike utilize the endless capacity of women to give themselves dutifully and passionately in a way which bears no relationship to the cash reward. Women's qualifications bear little relation too to their status at work. Men take over a large proportion of supervisory functions even in the women's professions like schoolteaching and social work. The fact that a large number of women work in these jobs makes relatively low pay socially acceptable. The human nature of the work is meant to provide enough compensation. On top of this women's role in the family is used as an excuse by employers for the low rates which characterize all 'women's work'. Women's liberation's emergence out of the student movement is itself an expression of the radicalizing contradictions faced by women who work in the consciousness industry.

Women are penalized for the essential work they do for capitalism at home in maintaining commodity producers. Women are held to be less capable than men, and less reliable. The absenteeism of young women with children is a frequent cause for complaint. In fact male absenteeism on the night shift in Britain is even higher. Absenteeism in both cases is an individual rebellion against capitalism's extraction of labour at the expense of personal life. Protective legislation originally intended as a defence against women exhausting themselves at home and at work, and to prevent them threatening men's jobs, has become a reason employers give for not paying women more. Although it doesn't apply to certain groups like women cleaners and can be got around even in factories, legislation preventing night work provides a minimal protection to women. There has been considerable pressure in Britain to abolish it. At Fords after the sewing machinists' strike in 1968 the employers offered equal pay if women would work the night shift. But the women rejected this because of the disruption it would cause to personal life.[12] Protective legislation against night work presents a difficult problem because it is grounds for discrimination against women within capitalism. Some women desperately need night work because they have young children and there are not enough nurseries. However, if the existing protections were abolished,

12. On the sewing machinists' strike see Sabby Sagall, 'Interview with Rose Boland', *Socialist Worker*, 21 September 1968, and John Matthews, *Ford Strike, The Workers' Story*, Panther, 1972, p. 54.

discrimination would simply take new forms. Agitation for improved working conditions, more nurseries, and leisure for both men and women is more likely to improve the life of women. Given the existing division of labour between the sexes the loss of protection at work would expose many women to intolerable pressure. Night work for men is inhuman enough, for women because of the double load of work and home it's even worse.

> Lynn Stevens works on the 10 p.m. to 6 a.m. shift at a light engineering factory in the East Midlands. She has two children, Elaine aged 8 and Mark aged 5 ... She felt one of the worst aspects of night work for women is that, whereas men on night work can often come home in the morning and go straight to bed, women started to do a 'bit of tidying or washing' and then found they only had time for a few hours sleep.
>
> 'I get so tired,' she said, 'and it's hard not to take it out on the children. I catch up at weekends. My husband helps me a lot. I think it's a disgrace for anybody to have to work nights. It destroys your life.'[13]

Because of this some trade unionists now are arguing that protective legislation should be extended to men, not abolished for women. It's not just that women work at home as well as outside, but that one job eats into the other. Women often take on routine work not because they are zombies but because they can't cope with the strain of double responsibility. A French working woman comments, 'If I had work where it was necessary to think all the time, my head would burst with all the preoccupations I have already.'[14]

It is apparent that the expansion in women's opportunities at work has not been a matter of linear progress but has come with changes in the structure of capitalist production. As new types of work have developed women have been employed where they were useful to employers. The fact that women in our society still have to keep the family going and are brought up to see themselves as sexual attachments to men, or as wives and mothers,

13. Valerie Clark, 'When Did You Last See Your Wife?', in *Socialist Worker*, 10 October 1970.

14. Quoted in Sullerot, *Histoire et sociologie du travail féminin*, Paris, 1968, p. 345.

has proved profitable to employers in certain trades. It has also given them an excuse to keep women amongst the unskilled and low-paid workers. It pays employers to section off particular workers and confine them to particular kinds of work. Awkward questions about low pay and bad conditions are thus avoided. The militancy of workers with experience in organizing can be offset by the employment of people with different attitudes to unions and work. Segmentation of the working class means that the militant and well-organized white males in expanding industries can be paid off and politically contained at the expense of other sections of the working class. This often leads to conflict between men and women workers because the men distrust the women's lack of wage militancy and the women resent the men getting more money than they do and won't support them. A very clear example of this appeared after the Leeds clothing strike a few years ago.[15]

The strike itself erupted in an enthusiastic and spontaneous manner with crowds of the predominantly female labour force pouring into meetings in halls, on grass verges outside factories, and busloads going off to the North-east to find young girls up there working for even lower pay than the Leeds women and with no union traditions. The strike was abruptly called off after negotiations between the trade union and the strike committee in which communists who'd been very active at first swung over to uphold the national agreements which had not calculated for the militancy shown by the women. Many of the women for whom the strike represented their first experience of industrial action were left bitter and disillusioned. Although more of them went to union meetings than before many were lost altogether. Nor could the consciousness which had begun to develop in the excitement of meetings, marches and fly-posted slogans extend to solidarity with the men. Some months after the militant feeling of the strike had died down the management sacked forty of the skilled men who had come out in support of the women. Every man was given £1000 redundancy pay to compensate. This seemed like an enormous sum to the women who were only

15. Information from an interview with Gertie Roche, a member of the Tailor and Garment Workers Union, Leeds, Spring 1971.

getting £11–£12 a week. For the first time they discovered the men were on £25 to £30 a week. The men had lost the whole of their livelihood and forfeited the chance to employ their craft skill ever again in the industry. But to the women it appeared differently. They refused to take action in support of the men and said to their stewards that the men should buy little shops and be grateful for what they could get.

Sometimes men are hostile to the women and gang up against them if their jobs are threatened. Because of the introduction of one-man buses, women bus conductresses, in one of the few jobs in which women have won equal pay, are going to become redundant because the men refuse to let them become drivers.[16] Men say women can't handle the heavy buses but admit they can deal with the little buses. In desperation early in 1969 a group of 25 women bus conductresses lobbied the conference of the Transport and General Workers Union which was discussing their right to be drivers. The delegates voted 35–33 against allowing the women into the meeting so the women occupied it during the lunch break. However, a resolution calling for women drivers from Southall bus garage was rejected on the grounds that it would lower the status of the job and put men out of work.[17] So the men now have the doubtful privilege of having to collect fares at the same time as driving the buses. Kath Fincham, one of the bus women involved, criticized the men's action. 'How can we expect to see greater democratic control for working people generally if there is no democracy within their own ranks? How can we expect to move forward in industry against the employers' undemocratic practices if you are not willing to support us in our struggle?'[18] It is apparent that only the employers benefit from these splits.

Trade unions play a dual role within capitalism. The official structure of the union is partially integrated into the state and enables the employer to calculate and plan, reducing spontaneous local militancy. But the union organization at the shop floor con-

16. *Women's Newspaper*, no. 2, London, 28 March 1971.

17. *Socialist Worker*, 25 January 1969.

18. Kath Fincham and Sabina Roberts, in *Socialist Woman*, May–June 1969.

tains an implicit attack on private profits and the control of capital over labour power. Centralization on a national level brings strength but it also means that the workers' creation, the union, can pass out of the control of the rank and file. This is particularly true of women because there are very few women represented at the top of unions and women are not often militantly organized at the base. Also the whole orientation of the trade unions is masculine. It is only by a special effort that men remember women. The only guarantee women have that their own interests will be considered is to organize as workers *and* as women.

The industrial militancy of women brings to the fore issues of democracy within the working-class movement. This is partly a matter between sections of the working class, the importance of solidarity between lower-paid and higher-paid workers, but it also involves sexual equality between male and female. Trade union women make these points again and again. Mrs C. E. Page from USDAW said at the Women's TUC conference in 1969,

> What is needed is a change in the whole attitude of society towards women. Until it is recognized that the working careers of women deserve to be provided for, just as much as those of men, there can be no real equality between men and women as workers. Some trade unionists are not guiltless, so far as discrimination against women is concerned.[19]

Other women put it in even stronger terms. By their failure to support women in their struggle for equal pay Miss J. O'Connell accused male trade unionists of condemning women to 'industrial apartheid'. Women, she said, had been 'fobbed off by pious resolutions, cosy chats and cups of tea in the House of Commons... We want more than the promise of a dream.'[20]

The men retort that women are notoriously apathetic about unions and refuse to stand up for themselves, to which the only reply is to return to the general situation of women in society. Trade union women have to combine militancy at work with housework, they often confront the unions as minorities who are

19. Mrs C. E. Page, USDAW, on Women Workers, TUC, 1969, p. 45.
20. Miss J. O'Connell, TUC, 1968, p. 455.

grossly under-represented on executives, and they are conditioned as women continually to defer to men.

Women are told so often that they are patient, conforming, modest, good at routine work and so on that in the end they come to believe it themselves; and a very useful belief it is for employers who want an uncomplaining work force slaving away unambitiously at routine work on low pay, and for those men – and there are many of them – who are afraid of female competition. One woman trade union official recently remarked that the problem with most women is not to make them work harder but to stop them breaking their backs for a pittance . . .

We have been relegated to subordinate work for so long that we have begun to develop inferiority complexes. James Baldwin once remarked in connection with racial discrimination that the white supremacists had only really succeeded when the oppressed people began to believe they were inherently inferior; in other words they began to accept the discriminators' view of themselves.[21]

Every woman in the labour force in capitalism doing 'women's work' has had the view of both male domination and the white ruling class imposed upon her. While women's position in the labour market is determined by their position as a group in production in the family, the nature of their exploitation at work is exactly the same as that of all lower-paid workers. Strategically it is only by organizing with other lower-paid workers that women will be able to raise their wages. But in terms of their consciousness they need to find a new notion of womanhood which will give them as a group the dignity and solidarity essential for industrial organization. This can come partly from work but it has to come also from all the other aspects of women's lives – all those moments of subjugation which contribute to hold women down, which men, including trade union men, ignore when they demand to be master in their own home.

But it is not simply that women are brought up to believe themselves inferior to men, it is also that they are socialized into a form of production in the family which is qualitatively different from production at work. In commodity production working-class women jostle against immigrant labour – North Africans

21. Mrs M. Turner, ASSET, Women Workers, TUC, 1969, p. 93.

in France, Portuguese in Germany, West Indian and Indian in Britain – and against black Americans in the USA. The complaints against both these immigrant workers and workers in the colonies are almost identical to the complaints against women.

> The workers, it is charged, 'show up late to work. They lack discipline, learn slowly, and don't stay on the job very long. They are not as good as white workers.' All of these characteristics are real enough but they are conditioned by the work-force experience of blacks and are reinforced within the context of secondary labour markets.[22]

Thus women, along with labour from the colonies and from the less developed capitalist countries, provide a reservoir of labour power. Despite the employers' complaints they are vital if capitalism is to contain the wage militancy of workers who have long since broken into the wage bargain, and who have learned to pay capital back with its own tricks. However, while capitalism makes use of non-capitalist attitudes to the work of women and immigrant workers, in certain sectors these don't pay. The more industrial concerns grow in size the more important it is for them to have completely reliable and disciplined workers. Spontaneity is even more dangerous for large firms than strong union organization. They prefer to know who they are bargaining with and want to tie workers down to long-term productivity deals which they are willing to combine with higher wage levels. For this reason the more progressive elements in the capitalist class are willing to countenance equal pay.

In Britain equal pay is scheduled for 1975. The original impetus behind the bill was the militancy of women on the shop floor. The Labour Government tried to forestall pressure from women building up in industry in order to satisfy equal pay demands in legislation. However, the terms on which equal pay will be granted – if at all – are vague. Certain experiences from other countries, the custom of simply defining jobs differently, the fact that so many women's jobs are not comparable to men's, the exclusion of women from jobs after they've got equal pay, indi-

22. William K. Tabb, *The Political Economy of the Black Ghetto*, W. W. Norton, New York, 1970.

cates that equal pay is far from being a panacea. A confidential document prepared by the Engineering Employers' Federation on equal pay[23] advises their members that they can avoid paying women the male rate by 'labour-saving machines, introducing job evaluation and having strict segregation of the sexes at the work place'. The report goes on to say that equal pay will mean a reassessment of the 'value' of employing women in certain jobs. 'Such questions as turnover rate, absenteeism, and reliability should be considered . . . The low salaries of female staff might have perpetuated a situation of over manning inefficiency and low productivity.'

Equal pay is also connected to job evaluation. The EEF describe this as 'a useful management tool for identifying the content and relative complexity of jobs and may assist management in rebutting unreasonable equal pay claims'.[24]

A certain uniformity and comprehensibility pays some sections of capitalism even at the expense of paying some workers a bit more – so long as they can recoup, of course, from within the firm. What they give the women they take from the men. Again the EEF report is straightforward on this. 'In particular the domestic male unskilled rate must be kept as low as possible to avoid unnecessarily increasing the costs of equal pay.'[25]

Equal pay within capitalism represents a rationalization of the work force which is comparable to the ending of slavery and serfdom. Although it is bitterly resisted by many employers and will be achieved only as a result of pressure, for the more dynamic sections of industry it could help to make them more efficient in the exploitation of both male and female labour power. It will also mean a real improvement on the miserable rates women get at present, as by raising the wages of women in jobs which are regarded as comparable to men's it will encourage other women to put a higher value on their labour and demand parity with

23. Quoted in *Socialist Worker*, 27 March 1971, pp. 4–5.

24. ibid.

25. ibid. A survey of 44 British firms in 1971 showed that already ways of avoiding implementing equal pay were in evidence. Some jobs were for women only and thus not comparable, other jobs were barred to women. *Sunday Times*, 21 November 1971.

other women. With equal pay too women will be clearly amongst the lower-paid work force rather than a specific category of labour employed as a 'favour' by capitalism. Equal pay once achieved will be a point to organize from – not a reason for ceasing to organize.

While equal pay represents the erosion of one of the barriers which has kept women from being fully integrated into the commodity system, many aspects of female consciousness will continue to reflect the features inherent in female production in the family. Rather than approaching women workers as 'backward' and seeking to correct their ideas we should learn from them the reasons behind attitudes. Sometimes women say 'Why should I join a union? I've never begged from anyone.' This kind of individual pride is a self-respect which comes from maintaining a home in isolation and making ends meet. But it can grow into a class pride which understands that going under is nothing to be ashamed of. Revolutionaries are dismissive of the aspirations of young working girls for marriage and children. But these longings, however domestic and limited, are still longings to relate to another person, and not to 'get on' or trample people down. When women are opposed to unions, equal pay or women's liberation, it is important to spend time in finding out why. It is nearly always because they have only known and understood them as alien, threatening forces which are likely to destroy the small bit of security and calm that exists in their lives. Precisely because working-class women are conditioned into notions of value and work which do not predominate within commodity production they see capitalism in a different way to their men.

Audrey Wise wrote to me, 'Women are sometimes less wage militant than men. This is not necessarily a reactionary thing. Though all men would say it is. It often derives from the fact that women place higher values than men on other job attributes, e.g. pleasant surroundings, nice people to work with, easy boss, opportunity to chat a bit, cleanliness of work place, bright decoration, "comfortable" job, etc. I say this is not necessarily reactionary, because it implies a search for human qualities in the job. Incidentally neither does it necessarily or even usually mean that wages are less necessary to the women than the men. Most women who work have a very definite strong financial necessity to do so. But men often sell themselves completely to the machines (e.g. give up tea-break, or take it standing without stopping the machine). Car workers earn big wages, but accept very dehumanizing working conditions. Sometimes this reluctance to measure everything by wages has the effect, at first sight strange and reactionary, of making women afraid of equal pay. I have examined the attitudes of many women on this and have come to find that this again is a reluctance to accept working conditions and arrangements which have been accepted by men. The great example is of course night work. And note that from this point of view night work as a nurse is quite different from night work in a factory. Night nursing is needed because the patients are people. Night factory work is needed to keep machines working. I find that attitudes of women often have a progressive human content which is completely unharnessed. Indeed it is completely unrecognized, because always looked at using male norms (even when looked at by progressive women, unfortunately). We live in a money society, where people are adjuncts to machines and their labour is a commodity. Refusal of women to adjust themselves to this point of view can have very progressive effects, but almost entirely unrealized so far.'

At one side we live in capitalism. To some extent we are forced to play along with the system in order to make life tolerable at all. We have to bargain within a particular historical situation and with opponents of flesh, blood and power. Equal pay is part of our bargain, more or less the least we expect within the system. We cannot afford the misconceived purity which does not go for immediate gains. But beyond just asking for more, if we are ever to end the spiralling whirlwind of simply economic inroads into the structure of capitalist society which are recouped by the political power of the ruling class, we need to develop notions of what an alternative society would be like. Similarly, the organization of women into trade unions is a necessary first step but women must also have control over union policy and make new forms of organizing which connect work and home. Simply because women have different expectations from men, simply because women have been kept out of certain areas of capitalism, they are well equipped to reach out to another form of social organization. They are able to see through some of the 'realities' men have come to regard as 'normal'. Capitalism itself has produced the contradictory need of being dependent on women's labour power in the home but in the process of its self-expansion seeking also to exploit women's labour in industry. It is up to us who want to transform the family and end the exploitation of all human beings to study carefully what is going on and use the knowledge we accumulate like a crowbar to crank open the tender and unprotected slits in Mr Moneybags's defences. Real unity between men and women can only come about by a clear and honest recognition of how capitalism has divided us. The contradictory encounter between the public sphere of labour and industry and the private family production of self and of goods and services for immediate use have made a new female consciousness possible. There is thus a new species of combined and uneven development at work, not between developed and underdeveloped countries, but between the dominant male mode of production, and the subordinate female family mode of production.

CHAPTER 7

Imperialism and Everyday Life

Capitalism is the first mode of economy with the weapon of propaganda, a mode which tends to engulf the entire globe and stamp out all other economies, tolerating no rival at its side. Yet at the same time it is also the first mode of economy which is unable to exist by itself, which needs other economic systems as a medium and a soil. Although it strives to become universal, and, indeed, on account of this its tendency, it must break down – because it is immanently incapable of becoming a universal form of production. In its living history it is a contradiction in itself, and its movement of accumulation provides a solution to the conflict and aggravates it at the same time. At a certain stage of development there will be no other way out than the application of socialist principles.

Rosa Luxemburg,
The Accumulation of Capital, 1963

The assumption Marx expressed in *Capital* – that the industrial revolution laid a 'new economical foundation for a higher form of the family, and of the relation between the sexes', because it assigned an important part in 'the process of production, outside the domestic sphere, to women, to young persons, and to children of both sexes', and that thus the 'capitalistic mode of exploitation' swept away 'the economical basis of parental authority'[1] – has remained only partially correct. He seemed to think that the family would simply be swept away along with other pre-capitalist preserves. Other factors have intervened to make the whole process more complicated. The family was supplemented rather than dis-

1. Marx, *Capital*, ed. D. Torr, Allen & Unwin, 1887, Vol. I, p. 498.

solved. Already in the nineteenth century the state had begun to take over certain aspects of the authority of individual families. The introduction of the Factory Acts meant that husbands could not benefit from their wives working in certain jobs, any more than parents could from their children's labour. The growth of compulsory education meant that parents retained economic control over their children but were answerable to the state legally if they kept them away from school. The pressure for these developments came from a varied lobby, from humane upper-class philanthropists, concerned about the destruction of old family ties and the horrors of the early stages of industrial revolution, from male workers concerned for their jobs, from the growing power of the labour movement, and finally from the needs of capitalism itself. As technology produced more and more complex machines in the twentieth century there was a need for a work force with some basic education. Similarly, industrialization demanded disciplined workers, broken in at an early age to specific modes of production and consumption. Schools for the working class developed round these narrow requirements of capitalist production. Legislation relating to children, child care, and family allowances have extended the state's intervention.

Despite these changes in capitalism, there was no need to alter fundamentally the division of labour between the sexes. The capitalist state has kept women morally responsible for children. Rather than turn the family into a rationalized part of commodity production, a baby farm with paid employees and no sentiment, it is both immediately more profitable and more politically convenient to utilize the accepted idea that women maintain the family outside the cash-nexus or at the lowest conceivable rate granted by the family allowance or social security. The continuance of such a state of affairs is directly linked to the unequal exploitation of female labour in industry. The tendency Marx observed for capitalism to throw up a whole range of new labour-intensive operations with every important technological advance makes this reserve army still essential despite automation. The position of women within the job structure has meant that the early Marxists' hope that female involvement in public production would create a proletarian consciousness has not been realized.

Instead working-class women have tended to maintain traces of pre-capitalist attitudes because of their responsibility for production in the family. The conflict Marx noted between work at home and in commodity production, the physical impossibility of women doing both, has not tended to lead to socialized schemes of child-rearing, except in wars. Ironically it is capitalist technology in the improvement of contraceptives which has reduced family size and made it possible for women who are married to work outside the home as well as in the family.

The appearance of new kinds of consumer products on a mass scale since the Second World War has created new patterns of demand and been the basis of the 'affluence' of the working class in the advanced capitalist countries. This itself is closely tied to married women working. By increasing productivity it has been possible to meet pressure from the labour movement for a higher standard of living. Some of the surplus extracted from the working class as a whole has been redistributed in the form of higher wages and welfare benefits. These welfare benefits again have contributed to the rearing of a healthier and consequently more efficient and 'socialized' wage-force. The gains of welfare thus have to be defended, but the social consequences are only incidentally helpful to people; their rationale is improved production. As the period of formal education has grown longer, the capital invested in children has risen. This has again further reduced the functions of the family but emphasized the need to preserve the nuclear family. Schools along with parents have also become crucial in the whole structure of conditioning agencies. There are indications that the unrespectable lower-working-class family is resistant to certain of the new characteristics of capitalist socialization. The peculiar demand of capitalism now is for workers who can use their initiative and discipline themselves from within, but are likely to consume without any worry in their leisure time.

Profits depend more and more on the efficient organization of work and on the 'self-discipline' of the workers rather than simply on speed-ups and other direct forms of increasing the exploitation of the workers. The family is therefore important both to shoulder the burden of the costs of education, and to carry out the repressive socialization of children. The family must raise children who have internalized hierarchical social relations, who will discipline themselves at work, efficiently without constant supervision ... Women are responsible for implementing most of this socialization.[2]

Thus capitalism has at the same time produced a need for women to socialize children at home and to use the labour of women in industry. It also needs the family as a market for consumer durables, and yet needs to preserve the image of the indispensable Mum in the traditional role of the housewife.

There are certain similarities to the contradictions generated in the imperial search for markets. In *The Accumulation of Capital* Rosa Luxemburg noted how capital in its search for expansion brought into being forces which were hostile to capitalism. At one side it needed to preserve non-capitalist sectors, but on the other it eroded these areas continually in the process of capital accumulation. 'The existence and development of capitalism requires an environment of non-capitalist forms of production, but not every one of these forms will serve its ends. Capitalism needs non-capitalist social strata as a market for its surplus value, as a source of supply for its means of production and as a reservoir of labour power for its wage system.'[3]

Non-capitalist economic organization develops on lines which do not always serve the needs of modern capitalism. 'A natural economy thus confronts the requirements of capitalism at every turn with rigid barriers. Capitalism must therefore always and everywhere fight a battle of annihilation against every historical form of natural economy that it encounters, whether this is slave economy, feudalism, primitive communism, or patriarchal peasant economy. The principal methods in this struggle are political force (revolution, war), oppressive taxation by the State, and cheap goods.'[4]

A similar imperialism has been mounted on the subordinate family mode of production. Like other subordinate modes, the

2. Peggy Morton, 'The Family under Capitalism', in *Leviathan*, May 1970.

3. Rosa Luxemburg, *The Accumulation of Capital*, Routledge & Kegan Paul, 1963, p. 368.

4. ibid., p. 369.

family has a slow rate of technological development and produces for an internal demand. There is little incentive to find new ways of doing things. The old ways are well enough. The family does not play an instrumental role in commodity production. The impact of commodity production has been to impose technological innovation on the family and to a lesser extent even onto the sexual act. Because of its need of a market for its goods capital increasingly penetrates areas of human life which were previously beyond the market. In the course of this penetration it disrupts and transforms them. Imperialism does not produce a series of little capitalisms which reproduce its own characteristics; it creates a curious kind of bastard society which is neither capitalist nor non-capitalist, but totally dependent on its continued exploitation by the capitalist mode of production. In the colonized countries raw materials and labour are extracted by the superior power of the imperialist. The introduction of mechanized products, and later mechanization, destroy native industries and traditional craft production. Peasant labour is brought into the towns and proletarianized. Attitudes to work change. Handwork is devalued and more efficient methods of organization introduced. The pattern of demand changes. People need the consumer goods from the advanced imperialist countries which they are unable to manufacture themselves. They become economically an appendage of imperialism. New ideas of status appear in which an imperial education and the possession of foreign consumer products are important. The new elites are their masters. Behind the superior technology is a superior military force, political expertise and a powerful propaganda machine. A colonial culture is brought into being and foisted upon the aspiring native. The victims of imperialism have three courses open to them, the unqualified acceptance of the invasion, a defensive rejection and retreat into the myths of a golden age, or a new revolutionary synthesis which combines elements of the previous non-capitalist economic forms with capitalist technology and in the process transforms both.

The family in its present form differs from non-capitalist countries, because it had no independent existence outside commodity production. The creation of a unit of direct production where services were exchanged, and labour power maintained for exploitation by capital, was part of the growth and development of capitalist social relations.

In the first stage of industrialization work was clearly separated from home and the sexual division of labour which already existed served to differentiate between male and female workers. Women formed a large reserve army useful for seasonal and irregular production. If unemployed they could be reabsorbed back into the family. Middle-class women were completely outside production. However, in the mid twentieth century women have become more closely integrated into the commodity system. Despite economic set-backs the demand for labour is consistent with the expansion of capital. Automation destroys some jobs, but like the early machines produces even more. Middle-class women have fought their way into production, and have thus penetrated into certain areas which were in the nineteenth century completely masculine.

Not only have women become more integrated into commodity production, but commodities have increasingly penetrated the home. This process has altered significantly the nature of female production in the home. The introduction of consumer substitutes for products formerly made in the family and the proliferation of gadgets to cut down on housework time have changed the nature of woman's work in the home. Thus the relationship between the subordinate mode of production, the family and the dominant commodity mode is altered. Because of the sexual division of labour, this disrupts the traditional contained role which capitalism created for women and means that the consciousness of women as a group starts to move.

The accomplishments of home production and the satisfactions of women's traditional sphere become intangible and fragmented. In the twentieth century the direct production work in the family has been undermined, not just by poverty as it was in the nineteenth century, but also by plenty. New ways of processing, preserving and selling food, new ways of storing food by refrigeration, mean that the nature of housework has become increasingly a service operation. The housewife maintains the male breadwinner and the children, not by producing goods herself, but by serving them with goods produced in the commodity system. Increasingly her only production work is the production of herself, as comforter, psychologist, or as sexual fantasy. The old criteria by which women could feel their value have thus gone without new ones really taking root. Women at home are confronting a devaluation of their house craft. Products like tinned and frozen food, machines for washing clothes or washing dishes, refrigerators, hoovers, mean that many household tasks become unnecessary. True, women can recapture their old craft skills in a culinary arts-and-crafts movement but this is dependent on leisure and wealth. You have to have time to hunt around in special shops for 'pure' ingredients. There is a rather hopeless last-ditch stand in home-baked bread and health foods. It is evident that such work is a matter of choice, not necessity. It assumes the character of a quaint pursuit, almost a hobby. The massed forces of the pre-packed sliced loaf – ideal for sandwiches at work – of the baked beans, the packaged soup, the frozen peas, the 'Smash' mash, the instant wonder cleaners and the handy mops assemble in the supermarket with history on their side. Goods from the commodity system reduce the *necessary* time spent in housework if not the actual time. Housework loses whatever point it ever had.

A similar imperial onslaught on sexuality, particularly female sexuality, has further eroded the traditional notions women had of their value. The cosmetics industry has mushroomed and created needs as well as products. The female who is the cosmetic ideal is more or less unattainable, no sooner captured she appears in another form. Playing on insecurity and anxiety the advertisers market goods which actually create new fears. Vaginal deodorants make people anxious about sexual odour. Acting on the assumption that women regard themselves through men's eyes as objects of pleasure, advertising and the media project a haunting and unreal image of womanhood. The persistent sense of dislocation between the unrealized female self and the projected female stereotypes has contributed to a feeling of failure. Women are not brought up to cope with the male world of production, work, ideas, power. They find their own preserved world threatened, their value reduced and depreciated, and are given an ideal of femininity which is foisted onto them by ever more powerful forms of the mass media.

The media have considerable power to throw back to us a version of ourselves which is presented as the 'norm'. This 'norm' is not unaffected by changes in society. Women's liberation has brought a sprinkling of adverts which attempt to appeal to dissatisfaction. However, the images of freedom are still completely male-defined. Either girls step out in freedom bras towards a man, or they simply become male fantasies of freedom. Girls replace men behind the wheels of fast sports cars. Advertising has a vested interest in presenting the sexual roles between men and women as clearly defined. But it has also to respond, however bizarrely, to changes in the consciousness of women. It reflects very clearly the production relations general in society. In order to sell commodities women are themselves reduced to commodities. However, if a section of middle-class women manage to alter their position in society through agitation there is no reason why adverts should not present these women with a spurious sense of liberation by inverting male–female roles in certain cases, and presenting men as commodities.

The visual impact of advertisements played a large part in awakening women to their own reflection in advanced capitalism. Immediate images on film and television make explicit areas of experience which have previously existed only in our subterranean selves. The very act of communication makes these sensations and experiences assume a shape, whereas before they were only implicit. New forms of consciousness are offered up by the marketing of new commodities and the mass communication of news and events. As a result, many aspects of life which were considered private and personal before become part of what is normally seen.

Sexual relations between men and women, or between men and men, and between women and women, are very clearly no longer exempt from the penetration of the market and the exposure of the sexual sell. This means that sexuality as the symbol of the natural assumes an importance beyond itself. It also means that political resistance to capitalism has to take on new forms, because the tendency for capitalism to distort all areas of human experience is no longer merely an abstract idea, it is an everyday happening.

Within advanced capitalism the maintenance of the separation of male and female conditioning has also assumed a new acuteness. This is partly because the existing sexual division of labour is still necessary to capitalist production. But also because of the deep and long-established nature of female subordination, and the hold it has over both men's and women's notions of their very identities, any challenge touches on deep and intensely personal areas of consciousness. The idea of romantic love, itself a creation of the bourgeoisie, has undergone innumerable transformations and permutations since it originated. Sexual love has assumed immense significance in containing many aspects of social relations incompatible with the work-discipline of commodity production. Here lurk affection, tenderness, passion, violence, satisfaction, fulfilment, excitement, imagination, religion, madness, fantasy, beauty, sensation, cruelty, transcendence, communion, escape. Weighed down with such unrealizable expectations, and surrounded by such an intolerable state of affairs elsewhere, sexuality has been as incapable as the family of providing a genuine alternative to the wasteland.

Sexual pleasure has an elusive and often exhausted quality. It is unable to compensate for everything denied to human beings in normal life. Not surprisingly it has assumed bizarre and distorted forms under the prevailing production for private profit. Belief in property, possession, domination does not stop at the factory gates. But like the family, sex represents the hope of an alternative. It has become the new 'sigh of the oppressed creature, the sentiment of a heartless world, and the soul of soulless conditions'. Like religion, which it rivals and replaces, sexuality now 'is the fantastic realisation of the human being in as much as the human being possesses no true reality'.[5] Love and orgasmic explosion have no proper place in a society in which the end of

5. Marx and Engels, *Gesamtausgabe*, I, 1, i, quoted in Karl Marx, *Selected Writings in Sociology and Social Philosophy*, ed. T. B. Bottomore and M. Rubel, Watts, 1956, pp. 26–7. See also Christopher Caudwell, 'A Study of Changing Values: Love', in *The Concept of Freedom*, Lawrence & Wishart, 1965.

life is the production of goods, in which work discipline as a thing in itself becomes the guardian of morality. Consequently sexual sensation is packaged, and delivered confined and synthesized in prevailing notions of sexuality – sugar sweet or black leather and net. Sex roles of dominator and dominated are part of the sexual sell. Such notions determine the structure of human fantasy – they are the symbol of everything which is not possible in everyday life.

Sexuality is communicated in the media in a series of images. A hand stroking hair, legs walking into summer, clean-washing-crisp housewives, children with cereal spoons and oral brand satisfactions, the power of money and class selling cigars, motor cars, pale ale – these become the visible shell for accumulated unrealizable desire. The loving emotion and physical excitement in sex become loaded with the great weight of this accumulation. Sexual relations between people start to sag, drop into odd places, assume fantastic shapes, in pornographic fetish, the rituals of desire, or the complacency of hypocritical virtue. Any challenge to the prevailing order of fantasy is a political struggle, just as the criticism of religion in the nineteenth century was political.

It would be foolish not to recognize the resilience of the subterranean imagination. The desecration of capitalism's sanctuaries, where pain and domination, grotesque imagination, masochism and guilt, emotional blackmail, and the thwarted ego have a hothouse life of their own, needs, as Wilhelm Reich understood, a conscious commitment to sexual alternatives in the revolutionary movement. Women's liberation attacked from the start the way in which women were presented in the media. By doing this the whole image of the family, of children, of manliness, became very obvious as well as the distortion of sexuality. The distortions appeared clearly because the old moral taboos were being eroded. Instead of the ethic of thrift, abstinence, and sacrifice which came out of the early stages of capital accumulation, capitalism needs now people who can regulate themselves precisely and on their own initiative at work and spend and consume without repression during their leisure. Though these long-term needs are temporarily contradicted by the creation of new forms of labour-intensive work which need the old kind of openly authoritarian supervision, and by short-term economic problems which involve cutting back on demand, they have already had a considerable social influence.

Much of the talk of permissive society and sexual liberation means merely permission to consume. However, this changing climate has a very important effect on the position of women. For the first time in human society it is possible for women to choose when they become pregnant. This with the panic about population explosion means that the persistent connection between sex and procreation, and the fear in male-dominated society of female sexual pleasure, and often of any sexual act which is not likely to produce children, lose their force to contain women – and men. The implications of these for both women's liberation and gay liberation are apparent.

Contraception, like other technological advances in capitalism, has a dual nature. By immeasurably increasing the possibilities of sexual relationship without fear of pregnancy, contraceptives contribute to a loosening of moral coercion to the 'permissive' society. Within such a society the carrot replaces the stick as the prime inducement to cooperation, though the stick is kept for the last resort. As long as sexuality, thus liberated, is confined to a small elite group, who are not within the discipline of commodity production, or as long as the kind of sexuality which is permitted retains, in however bizarre a form, the structure of dominance and abnegation, self-disgust and self-destruction, which within capitalism hold down and limit the human consciousness, it can be accommodated. But whenever the notion of pleasure takes off into a questioning of the need to produce people only to produce things it becomes subversive. Nasty, dirty hippy sex exults in its opposition to commodity production. It parades itself dancing in the streets, becomes gleefully transvestite, many coloured, confuses sexual roles, makes love every day. Then capitalism thinks 'how nice', not like those old-fashioned revolutionaries, and sells them a few clothes. The market flourishes and the fashion spreads. Nudity proliferates in the underground papers first, and then in the popular press. But despite its ambiguities, and particularly its ambiguities towards women, the emphasis in the underground on sexual pleasure still contains a threat to commodity production. When it seems to spread to the young working classes capitalism suddenly remembers morality, and in its zealous puritan disguise flays out against the sexuality it had formerly encouraged.

That the cult of free sex contains many distortions and much mystique and illusion is not surprising; what is surprising is the tendency for conservative supporters of capitalism to blame these on contraception, and look back longingly to the romantic nonsense of a mythical former unity, when pregnancy followed pregnancy, when childbirth frequently brought the mother's death, and infant mortality was high. The source of mystique and illusion comes from the mess outside, not from the technology of diaphragm, pill and safe abortion. Contraception, like any other kind of knowledge, is not accumulated in a social vacuum. The course of research by private firms, experiments with poor Third World women, the lack of concern about the effects on women psychologically and physically, reflect a bias which is profit-oriented, imperialist and male-biased. Women's liberation has consistently demanded abortion and contraception as means of control for women, not as part of a social engineering plan to keep population down to avoid the discontent of the poor. None the less, contraceptives lay the basis for a great explosion in the possibility of female pleasure. The release of the female orgasm from the fatalism, fear and shame of millennia is one of the triumphs of bourgeois technology. The social expression of this release and the shape it assumes in consciousness will depend on the activity of revolutionary human beings in history. Its integration is not impossible within capitalism. The glossy women's magazines are already pushing their own version of sexual liberation. How to undress in front of your husband, how to package yourself for all his sexual fantasies. In a popular book on sex technique published recently women are urged to work like the devil to accent their good features and hide the bad. They are shown how to package themselves for the market and check their tone and volume, to remember they are training their body to become a superb instrument of love. Passivity is rebuked, enthusiastic participation and a close check on 'Maintenance, Reclamation and Salvage' recommended.[6] But while increasing female participation in the sexual act is convenient as a compensatory feature of advanced capitalism, the notion of female power to control equally in bed upsets the conditioning of men to dominate and females to acquiesce. This is rather like the unresolved contradiction of how to educate people to work with initiative, and get them to continue to obey orders. Hysteria so long contained in the womb leaps exulting up from under. The female orgasm explodes and scrawls itself generously over the women's lavatory at Willesden railway station, 'We are all the same, good or bad, slag or vergin.'

6. 'J', *Sensuous Woman*, London, 1971, pp. 37–9. I owe this reference to Jenny Moss.

CHAPTER 8

Conclusion

Capitalism moves. The capitalist mode of production has penetrated farther and deeper than any other form of production. Geographically it has extended its technology in search of markets; politically it has devised the most ingenious methods of control in its own interests; economically it has created means of production which are wonderful in their productive capacity and terrifying in their devastation. Its industry has devoured human labour power and human intelligence. In its search for raw materials it has laid waste the land and is beginning to exhaust even the sea. Worse, its version of itself has entered the souls and spirits of millions of men and women, so we no longer know what is our own and what is alienated to capital.

This indiscriminate hunger of capital destroys but it also provokes resistance. The antagonisms it generates produce the shifts and fissures which make the growth of new movements possible. In quiet times the hope of liberation grows lichen-like on the inhospitable rock. In times of upheaval the new growths can take root.

In order to change capitalism we have to understand how it is made, how it moves and how it came into being. We have to see how it is different from, or related to, other forms of production, how it is hinged together. It is a foxy old thing, wily at dealing with the opposition it brings into being, whether its opponent is the working class or movements for black or women's liberation.

We have to start off where we came in. The predicament of being born a woman in capitalism is specific. The social situation of women and the way in which we learn to be feminine is peculiar to us. Men do not share it, consequently we cannot be simply included under the general heading of 'mankind'. The only claim that this word has to be general comes from the dominance of men in society. As the rulers they presume to define others by their own criteria.

Women are not the same as other oppressed groups. Unlike the working class, who have no need for the capitalist under socialism, the liberation of women does not mean that men will be eliminated. Sex and class are not the same. Similarly people from oppressed races have a memory of a cultural alternative somewhere in the past. Women have only myths made by men.

We have to recognize our biological distinctness but this does not mean that we should become involved in an illusory hunt for our lost 'nature'. There are so many social accretions round our biology. All conceptions of female 'nature' are formed in cultures dominated by men, and like all abstract ideas of human nature are invariably used to deter the oppressed from organizing effectively against that most unnatural of systems, capitalism.

The oppression of women differs too from class and race because it has not come out of capitalism and imperialism. The sexual division of labour and the possession of women by men predates capitalism. Patriarchal authority is based on male control over the woman's productive capacity, and over her person. This control existed before the development of capitalist commodity production. It belonged to a society in which the persons of human beings were owned by others. Patriarchy, however, is contradicted by the dominant mode of production in capitalism because in capitalism the owner of capital owns and controls the labour power but not the persons of his labourers.

What form female oppression took in the distant past is impossible to verify and the search for it rapidly becomes a chimerical pursuit of origins. We can only guess that the physical weakness of women and the need of protection during pregnancy enabled men to gain domination.

More relevant to us are the consequences of opposing a form of oppression which has taken a specific shape in capitalism, but which nevertheless existed in precapitalist society. In order to act effectively we have to try to work out the precise relationship between the patriarchal dominance of men over women, and the property relations which come from this, to class exploitation and racism.

Conclusion

In order to understand the traces of patriarchy which have persisted into the present, it is essential to see what part patriarchy played in precapitalist society. The dominance of men over women in the past was more clearly a property relation than it is now. We usually think of property as things. However, animals and people can also be possessions. The word 'stock' still covers the breeding of animals and people as well as assets on the stock exchange. But women are no longer so clearly means of production owned by men. When a man married in a society in which production was only marginally beyond subsistence, he married a 'yoke-fellow' whose labour was crucial if he were to prosper. Her procreative capacity was important not only because of the high infant mortality rate but also because children meant more hands to labour. The wife's role in production was much greater because although tasks were already sexually divided many more goods were produced in the household. Women who were too high up in the social scale to work with their own hands supervised household production.

The family was a collective working group. The father was its head, but for survival the labour of wife and children was necessary. Notions of leisure were necessarily restricted in a situation of scarcity when the surplus produced was very small. Consequently, the economic and social cohesion of the family was more important than what individuals in the family might want or regard as their right. Indeed the notion that women and children had individual interests which could not be included in those of the father is a modern concept that belongs to capitalism. It would have seemed bizarre, atomistic and socially destructive in earlier times. The productive forces of capital thus made the concept of individual development possible even though it was still confined in practice to the lives of those who belonged to the dominant class.

The introduction of individual wages and the end of the ownership of people in serfdom did not dissolve the economic and social control of men over women. The man remained the head of the family unit of production and he retained control over the ownership of property through primogeniture. Both his wife's capacity to labour and her capacity to bear his children were still part of his stock in the world. Moreover, the notion that this was part of the order of things was firmly embedded in all political, religious and educational institutions.

Although capitalism temporarily strengthened the control over women by the middle- and upper-class men in the nineteenth century by removing them from production, it has tended to whittle away at the economic and ideological basis of patriarchy. As wage labour became general and the idea spread in society that it was unjust to own other people, although the exploitation of their labour power was perfectly fair, the position of the daughter and the wife appeared increasingly anomalous. Ironically, middle-class women came to the conviction that their dependence on men and the protection of patriarchal authority were intolerable precisely at a time when the separation of work from home was shattering the economic basis of patriarchy among the working class. The factories meant that the economic hold of men over women in the working-class family was weakened. Machinery meant that tasks formerly done by men could be done by women. The woman's wage packet gave her some independence. Ideologically, however, men's hold persisted among the workers and was nurtured by the male ruling class.

Subsequently by continually reducing the scope of production, by developing the separation between home and work, and by reducing the time spent in procreation, a great army of women workers has been 'freed' for exploitation in the commodity system. This integration of married women into the labour market has been especially noticeable in the advanced capitalist countries since the Second World War and testifies to the tendency for capital to seek new reserves of labour. The result in terms of women's consciousness at work is only now beginning to be felt. While the dissolution of the extended kinship networks has produced in the nuclear family a streamlined unit suitable for modern capitalism, it has forced an examination of the relationships of man to woman and parent to child.

The struggle of the early feminist movement for legal and political equality and the assumptions it has bequeathed to women now, despite the degeneration of its radical impulse, have strained the hold of patriarchy in the capitalist state, though without dislodging it. The power of the working class within capitalism and the growth of new kinds of political movements recently, particularly for black liberation, have touched the consciousness of women and brought many of us to question the domination of men over women. This has taken a political shape, in the new feminism of women's liberation.

The development of contraceptive technology in capitalism means that ideas of sexual liberation can begin to be realized. The fact that sexual pleasure now need not necessarily result in procreation means a new dimension of liberation in the relation of men and women to nature is possible. It also removes some of patriarchy's most important sanctions against rebellion. The right to determine our own sexuality, to control when or if we want to give birth, and to choose who and how we want to love are central in both women's liberation and in gay liberation. All these are most subversive to patriarchy.

However, although capitalism has itself eroded patriarchy and has brought into being movements and ideas which are both anti-capitalist and anti-patriarchal, it still maintains the subordination of women as a group. Patriarchy has continued in capitalism as an ever present prop in time of need. Although women are not literally the property of men, the continuation of female production in the family means that women have not yet even won the right to be exploited equally. The wage system in capitalism has continued to be structured according to the assumption that women's labour is worth half that of men on the market. Behind this is the idea that women are somehow owned by men who should support them. Women are thus seen as economic attachments to men, not quite as free labourers. Their wage is still seen as supplementary. If a woman has no man she is seen as a sexual failure and the inference is often that she is a slut as well. She also has to struggle to bring up a family alone, on half a man's income. This very simple economic fact about the position of women in capitalism acts as a bribe to keep women with men: it has no regard for feeling or suffering and makes a mockery of any notion of choice or control over how we live. It also means that women make up a convenient reserve army which will work at half pay and can be reabsorbed back into the family if there is unemployment.

Our sexual conditioning means that we submit more readily than men to this intolerable state of affairs. We are brought up to think not only that it is just that the private owner of capital can extract profit from the surplus we produce but also that it is legitimate for the capitalist to return to us in the form of wages about half the sum he has to pay a man. Equal pay is obviously only the beginning of an answer to this – though even the chances of the limited measures in the Equal Pay Act in Britain look doubtful if the Tories have their way. The inequality of women at work is built into the structure of capitalist production and the division of labour in industry and in the family. The equality of women to men, even the equal *exploitation* of women in capitalism, would require such fundamental changes in work and at home that it is very hard to imagine how they could be effected while capitalism survives.

Our labour in the family goes unrecognized except as an excuse to keep us out of the better jobs in industry and accuse us of absenteeism and unreliability. This separation between home and work, together with the responsibility of women for housework and child care, serves to perpetuate inequality. Women, as a group in the labour force, are badly paid and underprivileged. This is not only economically profitable to capitalism, it has proved a useful political safety valve. There are many aspects of women's consciousness which have never fully come to terms with the capitalist mode of production. There is no reason why these should not take a radical and critical form in the context of a movement for liberation but in the past they have been used against women and against the working class. It is quite handy for capitalism if wives can be persuaded to oppose their husbands on strike, or if men console themselves for their lack of control at work with the right to be master in their own home. When this happens patriarchy is earning its keep. Similarly, when men and women do not support each other at work both patriarchy and capitalism are strengthened.

Because production in the family differs from commodity

production we learn to feel that it is not quite work. This undermines our resentment and makes it harder to stress that it should be eliminated as much as possible not only by technology but by new styles of living, new buildings, and new forms of social care for the young, the sick and the old.

In capitalism housework and child care are lumped together. In fact they are completely different. Housework is drudgery which is best reduced by mechanizing and socializing it, except for cookery, which can be shared. Caring for small children is important and absorbing work, which does not mean that one person should have to do it all the time. But we are taught to think there is something wrong with us if we seek any alternative. The lack of nurseries and of other facilities for children and the rigid structuring of work and the division of labour between the sexes again makes choice impossible.

Propaganda about our feminine role helps to make us accept this state of affairs. Values linger on after the social structures which conceived them. Our ideas of what is 'feminine' are a strange bundle of assumptions, some of which belong to the Victorian middle class and others which simply rationalize the form patriarchy assumes in capitalism now. Either way the notion of 'femininity' is a convenient means of making us believe submission is somehow natural. When we get angry we are called hysterical.

Thus, although capitalism has eroded the forms of production and property ownership which were the basis of patriarchy, it has still retained the domination of men over women in society. This domination continues to pervade economic, legal, social and sexual life.

It is not enough to struggle for particular reforms, important as these are. Unless we understand the relationship of the various elements within the structure of male-dominated capitalism, we will find the improvements we achieve are twisted against us, or serve one group at the expense of the rest. For example, the wider dissemination of contraceptive information and the weakening of guilt about our sexuality have meant a major improvement in the lives of many women. However, the removal of fear alone is not enough because relations between the sexes are based on the ownership of property, property consisting not only of the woman's labour in procreation, but also of her body. Therefore, while class, race and sex domination remain a constituent element of relations between men and women, women and women, and men and men, these relations will continue to be distorted. Sexual liberation in capitalism can thus continue to be defined by men and also continue to be competitive. The only difference between this and the old set-up is that when patriarchy was secure men measured their virility by the number of children they produced, now they can apply more suitable means of assessing masculinity in a use-and-throw-away society and simply notch up sexual conquests.

There are other examples of feminist reforms being distorted by the structure of capitalist society. We are far from the situation of baby farms and state-controlled breeding but these are the lines along which a pure capitalism, shorn of the remnants of earlier forms of production, would develop. Similarly, one group of women can be bought off at the expense of another, young women against old, middle class against working class. If we are ready to settle for a slightly bigger bite of the existing cake for a privileged section we will merely create gradations among the underprivileged. We will not change the context in which women are inferior. For instance, in Britain there has been some recent discussion about giving women better jobs in management and promoting secretaries because they will work harder for less pay.

Capitalism is not based on the organization of production for people but simply on the need to secure maximum profit. It is naïve to expect that it will make exceptions of women. It is impossible now to predict whether capitalism could accommodate itself to the complete elimination of all earlier forms of property and production and specifically to the abolition of patriarchy. But it is certain that the kind of accommodation it could make would provide no real solution for women when we are unable to labour in commodity production because we are pregnant: socially helpless people protected in capitalism are not only treated as parasites who are expected to show gratitude but are under the direct power of the bourgeois state. Also class and race cut across sexual oppression. A feminist movement which is confined to the specific oppression of women cannot, in isolation, end exploitation and imperialism.

We have to keep struggling to go beyond our own situation. This means recognizing that the emphases which have come out of women's liberation are important not only to ourselves. The capacity to bring into conscious combination the unorganizable, those who distrust one another, who have been taught to despise themselves, and the connection which comes out of our practice between work and home, personal and political, are of vital significance to other movements in advanced capitalism. Similarly, the comprehension in women's liberation of the delicate mechanism of communication between the structures of capitalist society and the most hidden part of our secret selves is too important not to become part of the general theory and practice of the Left. Women's liberation has mounted an attack on precisely those areas where socialists have been slow to resist capitalism: authoritarian social relationships, sexuality and the family. 'Personal' relations within capitalism, where the labour force is reproduced, are becoming increasingly crucial in the modern organization of industry. We have to struggle for control not merely over the means of production but over the conditions of reproduction.

The predicament of working-class women is the most potentially subversive to capitalism because it spans production and reproduction, class exploitation and sex oppression. The movement of working-class women is thus essential for the emergence of socialist feminism because the necessary connections are forced upon women who are working-class when they take action. When they occupy or strike they have their own conditioning as women, the attitude of husbands, the care of the family, the sexual patronage of union officials, the ridicule of the popular press about petticoat pickets and Mrs Mopps, the overwhelming contempt from the middle class for their sex and their class. They are thus compelled to develop both sisterhood and solidarity or be crushed. They need each other, they need the support of male workers, and their fight at work connects immediately to their situation at home. Their organization and militancy is vital not only for women's liberation but for the whole socialist and working-class movement.

The problem about how a revolutionary theory can come out of a day-to-day practice defined by the existence of capitalism has long bedevilled revolutionary socialism. The concept of the Leninist party as the conscious embodiment of an alternative has become dubious, because the party in reality will still express the viewpoint of sections which are the stronger within capitalism, most obviously men, for example. Moreover, the party itself can become absorbed in the immediate problem of surviving within capitalism rather than in the task of exposing contradictions and seeking revolutionary transformation. The mobilization of new groups within capitalism against a specific form of oppression is thus very important, but more important still is the means of translating the experience of one group to another without merely annexing the weaker to the stronger.

Thus it is not just groups which have a position of power at the point of production in the advanced sectors of the capitalist economy, but the organization of groups whose consciousness spans several dimensions of oppression which becomes crucial in a revolutionary movement.

This is not an idealization of weakness. Women as a group are extremely vulnerable within capitalism, but because of our social situation we are forced to find the means of going beyond our own specific oppression. The blocks against us are very real; male domination permeates every organization within capitalism including trade unions and revolutionary groups, and the problem of how to safeguard our autonomy while making a strategy of organizing with men is a persistent dilemma in the women's movement.

Nor is this an evasion of the urgent problem of making an offensive organization which is capable of overcoming the tremendous resources of the advanced capitalist state. The substitution of the women's movement for such an organization would be most evidently absurd. Although we have the capacity to go beyond our own predicament, and although alternatives must be continually drawn out of our day-to-day struggle to defend women against capitalism, neither our structure, nor our politics, are the same as those of a revolutionary organization. We come into women's liberation out of our specific predicament as women, not as people who necessarily are committed to the creation of socialism. We are, moreover, essentially a partial organization representing a specific group. Such a substitution is both dishonest and foolhardy. It implies imposing a consciousness on other women and exposing ourselves to the full repression of the state.

There are no short-cuts. The making of a revolutionary socialist organization which is capable of taking the offensive without being either absorbed or smashed, which can at once safeguard the interests of the groups within it and not simply reproduce the structures of authority and domination which belong to capitalism, is a gigantic task. Autonomy and cohesive organization in the face of repression go uncomfortably together. The models of the past can help us but do not fit the special problems of the modern capitalist state. However, the political process of making an effective movement for the liberation of women – which means a movement in which working-class women are in the majority – is an essential part of this task.

List of Recent Publications

Some of the pamphlets, journals and books referred to in the text are not generally available in most commercial bookshops or in libraries. Although some may be out of print, here are the publication addresses. Try the British Museum for the publications which have ceased.

For a list of books included in the text and others, see Sheila Rowbotham, 'Women's Liberation and Revolution', Falling Wall.

Body Politic	Stage I 21 Theobalds Road London WC1X 8SL
Bread and Roses	1145 Massachusetts Avenue Cambridge, Mass 02139, USA
Enough	Bristol Women's Liberation Group Wellington Buck 21 Canynge Road Bristol 8
Falling Wall Press	79 Richmond Road Montpelier Bristol BS6 5EP
Germ's Eye View	ceased publication
International Socialism Pamphlets	Corbridge Works Corbridge Crescent London E2 9DS
I.S. Women's Newsletter	ceased publication
now *Women's Voice*	Corbridge Works Corbridge Crescent London E2 9DS
Leviathan	ceased publication
Monthly Review	116 West 14th Street New York, NY 10011, USA
New England Free Press	791 Tremont Street Boston, Mass 02118, USA

List of Recent Publications

New Left Review	7 Carlisle Street London W1
Partisans	1 Place Paul-Painlevé Paris 5e, France
Radical America	1237 Spaight Street Madison, Wisconsin 53703, USA
Seven Days	ceased publication
Shrew	Women's Liberation Workshop 38 Earlham Street London WC2
Socialist Woman	182 Pentonville Road London N1
Socialist Worker	Corbridge Works Corbridge Crescent London E2 9DS
Spokesman Pamphlets	Partisan Press Bertrand Russell House Gamble Street Nottingham NG7 4ET
The Irrational in Politics	Solidarity Pamphlet No. 33 c/o H. Russell 53A Westminster Road Bromley, Kent
Women: A Journal of Liberation	3028 Greenmount Avenue Baltimore, Maryland 21218, USA
Women Now	Nottingham Women's Liberation Group 85 Rivermead Wilford Lane West Bridgford Nottingham

Since I wrote *Woman's Consciousness, Man's World*, there has been considerable discussion in women's liberation and gay liberation about the creation of a new consciousness, the role of the family and women's position in relation to the trade unions. I have listed some of these so anyone interested can follow up specific questions I have touched upon, and trace the various currents of, ideas in the women's movement.

The Creation of a New Consciousness

'Anaïs Nin and the Identity of Women' by Carol Morrell in *Women Speaking*, Jan–March 1973 (20p)

The Wick
Roundwood Avenue
Hutton
Brentwood, Essex

Books, Spring 1973, No. 11
includes Margaret Drabble, Jeni Couzyn, Michelene Wandor, Fleur Adcock, Susan Hill: on women and writing

7 Albermarle Street
London W1V 4BB

'Notes on Women's Cinema', *Screen*, Pamphlet 2 (25p)
includes Claire Johnston, Naome Guilbart, Nelly Kaplin, Barbara Halpen Martineau: on women's cinema

Television
63 Old Compton Street
London W1V 5PN

'From Tribal Kitchen Sink to Dishwasher' by Michelene Wandor, in *Red Rag* (10p)

96 Grove Road
London N12 9EA

'Ultimate Goals' by Angela Hamblin in *Woman's Liberation Review*, Oct. 1972 (20p), on male and female culture

27 Deeds Grove
High Wycombe
Bucks.

The Family

Marxism Today, Autumn–Spring 1972–73: discussion on the family; there have been a series of articles in the various issues of the journal (20p each)

Central Books
37 Gray's Inn Road
London WC1X 8PS

New Edinburgh Review, No. 18, 1972 (15p) includes Margaret Dickinson on 'Sex Differences and Society', Sara Delamont on 'Fallen Engels', Sue Sharpe on 'The Role of the Nuclear Family in the Oppression of Women', Elizabeth Wilson on 'Sexual Oppression'

1 Buccleuch Place
Edinburgh EH8 9LW

List of Recent Publications

The Politics of Homosexuality by Don Milligan (20p)	Pluto Press 10 Spencer Court 7 Chalcot Road London NW1 8LH
'Sexism, Capitalism and the Family' by Rosalind Delmar in *Radical Philosophy* (25p)	c/o Richard Norman Darwin College The University Canterbury, Kent
Socialist Woman, Jan–Feb 1973 includes review of 'The Power of Women' and the 'Subversion of the Community'	182 Pentonville Road London N1
Women and the Subversion of the Community: A Woman's Place by Mariarosa Dalla Costa and Selma James (25p)	Falling Wall Press 79 Richmond Road Montpelier Bristol BS6 5EP

Work and Trade Unions

The Choice Before Us: discussion of Selma James's *Women the Unions and Work* (5p)	An I.M.G. Publication 182 Pentonville Road London N1
Red Rag No. 2: contains several articles on Selma James's *Women the Unions and Work* (10p)	9 Stratford Villas London NW1
'Trying to Stay Human' by Audrey Wise in *Red Rag* No. 3 (10p) This issue also includes Jean French and Fay Pedder on women in trade unions.	(address as above)
'Women and the Struggle for Workers' Control' by Audrey Wise, in *Spokesman Pamphlet* No. 33 (12p)	Partisan Press Bertrand Russell House Gamble Street Nottingham NG7 4ET
Women the Unions and Work: or What is Not to be Done by Selma James (10p)	Crest Press 154 Ladbroke Grove London W10
Women Workers in Britain: A Handbook (25p), by Leonora Lloyd	Socialist Woman 182 Pentonville Road London N1

General

The Body Politic: Women's Liberation in Britain 1969–1972 includes articles on the family, housework, work, trade unions, sexuality (60p)	Stage I Theobalds Road London WC1X 8SL
Thoughts on Feminism in Radical Feminists (7p) sections on men, reproduction, family, women's culture	Women's Liberation Workshop (new address coming)
Women Fight Back by Kath Ennis (10p)	I. S. Women Corbridge Works Corbridge Crescent London E2 9DS

This is not a full list of women's liberation publications. It will inevitably also be out of date by the time this book is published.

Women's Liberation Workshop in London keep a stock of current pamphlets. You can also find them at Collet's Bookshop on Charing Cross Road and in Compendium, Camden Town. If you order copies by post, remember to include postage.

Index

Index

MORE ABOUT PENGUINS, PELICANS, PEREGRINES AND PUFFINS

For further information about books available from Penguins please write to Dept EP, Penguin Books Ltd, Harmondsworth, Middlesex UB7 ODA.

In the U.S.A.: For a complete list of books available from Penguins in the United States write to Dept DG, Penguin Books, 299 Murray Hill Parkway, East Rutherford, New Jersey 07073.

In Canada: For a complete list of books available from Penguins in Canada write to Penguin Books Canada Ltd, 2801 John Street, Markham, Ontario L3R 1B4.

In Australia: For a complete list of books available from Penguins in Australia write to the Marketing Department, Penguin Books Australia Ltd, P.O. Box 257, Ringwood, Victoria 3134.

In New Zealand: For a complete list of books available from Penguins in New Zealand write to the Marketing Department, Penguin Books (N.Z.) Ltd, Private Bag, Takapuna, Auckland 9.

In India: For a complete list of books available from Penguins in India write to Penguin Overseas Ltd, 706 Eros Apartments, 56 Nehru Place, New Delhi 110019.

Also by Sheila Rowbotham

WOMEN, RESISTANCE AND REVOLUTION

'The liberation of women necessitates the liberation of all human beings.'

In *Women, Resistance and Revolution* Sheila Rowbotham has produced a wide-ranging survey of the roots of inequality and of the long but sporadic struggle to overcome it. Her narrative extends from the seventeenth century to the Vietnamese War, showing how certain women have struggled, in both revolutionary and repressive situations, to achieve liberation.

Revolutionary thought has been slow to accept the validity of feminism, regarding it as a limiting and reformist movement which can only distract from the main area of struggle. Sheila Rowbotham here forces a re-evaluation of the relationship between women's liberation and the revolutionary left. Her book is one in which, as she says, 'feminism and Marxism come home to roost. They cohabit in the same space somewhat uneasily . . . They are at once incompatible and in real need of each other.'

'Essential reading . . . Miss Rowbotham has succeeded in that difficult feat – the combining of carefully researched political writing with a deep humanity' – Jill Tweedie in the *Guardian*

Also published in Penguins

DOUBLE IDENTITY

The Lives of Working Mothers

Sue Sharpe

What does going out to work mean to working mothers?

It is only too easy to accept an image of working mothers as weary, harassed women dashing from home to work and back in order to earn money to support the family. This picture, however, is far from complete, as the mothers contributing to this book illustrate. Although a woman's income is often essential to maintain family living standards, and it is tiring to organize a job, home and family, working can also affect a woman's life in very positive ways. It can enhance her self-image, provide a sense of economic independence and a separate identity, and improve relationships within the family.

Sue Sharpe talked to mothers living in different parts of Britain and working in a variety of jobs using their experiences, she explores both the practical complexities of combining work and motherhood, and the economic, social and psychological meaning of work in women's lives.

Also published in Penguins

THE SCEPTICAL FEMINIST

A Philosophical Enquiry

Janet Radcliffe Richards

What should feminists be fighting for?

In this important and original study, Janet Radcliffe Richards demonstrates with incisive, systematic and often unexpected arguments the precise nature of the injustice women suffer, and exposes the fallacious arguments by which it has been justified. Her analysis leads her to considerable criticism of many commonly held feminist views, but from it emerges the outline of a new and more powerful feminism which sacrifices neither rationality nor radicalism.

'A superb piece of applied philosophy, the arguments clear and cogent, the writing lucid and elegant' – *The Times Literary Supplement*

WOMEN, SEX AND PORNOGRAPHY

Beatrice Faust

What do women think of pornography?

Pornography is a topic that produces feverish responses, but women's reactions until now have been left unexamined. Even the responses of the women's movement have been contradictory. In this major new work, Beatrice Faust discusses the psychology of sexual differences and how they relate to differences in the sexual and erotic styles of men and women and the influence of culture.

In a frank and polemical analysis, Beatrice Faust explores the enormous social implications of these sexual differences, from novels, films and fashion to social behaviour patterns – and rape. She argues that pornography is neither pro- nor anti-woman. But it certainly presents a misleading view of woman's sexuality, and the solution is not censorship but sex education through bona fide erotica and the recognition of differences between male and female sexuality.

Also published in Penguins

FROM HERE TO MATERNITY

Ann Oakley

What is it *really* like having a baby?

We know what the experts think it should be like, but this book gives a voice to women who are able to describe the real experience. Using the tape-recorded words of sixty women, it gives an authentic account of how first-time mothers react to the various stages of pregnancy, birth and baby care.

Dr Oakley discusses whether or why women want to become pregnant in the first place; how they recognize their condition and have it medically confirmed; how women imagine motherhood to be; what the birth is actually like; the way mothers feel about their new-born babies; the return from hospital; post-natal depression; the emotive topic of how babies ought to be, and are, fed; becoming a father; mothers' routines etc.

This important book shows that most women are unprepared for the pain and shock of birth or for the hard, selfless and lonely work of looking after a baby. But it shows, too, that the baby provides compensations – even if these are not of the romantic story book variety.

and

HOUSEWIFE

The Pelican Marx Library

Published in association with New Left Review

GRUNDRISSE

Foundations of the Critique of Political Economy
(Translated with a foreword by Martin Nicolaus)

EARLY WRITINGS

(Introduced by Lucio Colletti; translated by Rodney Livingstone and Gregory Benton)

THE REVOLUTIONS OF 1848

Political Writings – Volume 1
(Edited and introduced by David Fernbach)

SURVEYS FROM EXILE

Political Writings – Volume 2
(Edited and introduced by David Fernbach)

THE FIRST INTERNATIONAL AND AFTER

Political Writings – Volume 3
(Edited and introduced by David Fernbach)

CAPITAL

VOLUME 1
(Introduced by Ernest Mandel; translated by Ben Fowkes)

VOLUME 2
(Introduced by Ernest Mandel; translated by David Fernbach)

VOLUME 3
(Introduced by Ernest Mandel; translated by David Fernbach)